THE
BRITISH HOUᴗᴗᴡᴉᴦᴇ

Mrs Martha Bradley's *British Housewife* was first published in weekly parts in 1756, then issued as a two-volume set that same year or the next. This facsimile edition is also divided, but into six, not two, volumes. As the original is itself divided into monthly chapters, this arrangement works satisfactorily.

THE
BRITISH HOUSEWIFE:
OR, THE
COOK, HOUSEKEEPER's,
AND
GARDINER's COMPANION.

By

Mrs. MARTHA BRADLEY, late of BATH
(1756)

A FACSIMILE EDITION

VOLUME III
April, May

PROSPECT BOOKS
1997

First published in Great Britain in 1997, by Prospect Books,
Allaleigh House, Blackawton, Totnes, Devon TQ9 7DL.

British Library Cataloguing in Publication Data
A catalogue record of this book is available from the British Library.

ISBN 0907325688
ISBN 0907325637 in respect of the whole set

Printed by Antony Rowe Ltd, Bumper's Farm, Chippenham,
Wiltshire SN14 6QA.

CONTENTS

* Sections III–VIII are numbered in error in the text as Sections II–VII.
† Sections IX and X are numbered in error in the text as Sections VII and VIII.

SUBSCRIBERS TO THIS PRESENT EDITION

Priscilla Bain
Peter Brears
Alan Brown
Kit Chapman
Mrs K.M. Charlton
Covington & Burling
Mrs G.M. Cox
Caroline Davidson
Ove Fosså
Mr R.A. Grant
Dr E.S. Halberstadt
Geraldene Holt
Lynette Hunter
Mr S.H. Jollye
Katherine Knight
James Lamb
Fiona Lucraft
Reinhard Madlinger
Laura Mason
Mrs M.B. Maunsell
Pat & Jim McLavey
Stephen & Barbara Mennell
Michael & Joy Michaud
Joan Morgan

Pam Musa
Julia Neville
Elizabeth Orange
Helen Pollard
Dr Esteban Pombo-Villar
Dermod Quirke & Brian Holser
The Reform Club
Mrs U.A. Robertson
Liz Seeber
Roy Shipperbottom
Mrs A.S.M. Smith
Mr D.R. Smith
Liz Calvert Smith
Professor R.J. Theodoratus
Malcom Thick
Gordon J. Van der Water
Bas van Oosterhout
Harlan Walker
Dr & Mrs R.J. Webber-Hill
Robin Weir
Barbara Ketcham-Wheaton
Dr Eileen White
Chris Young & Verni Tannam

THE
BRITISH HOUSEWIFE:
OR, THE
COOK, HOUSEKEEPER's,
AND
GARDINER's COMPANION.

CALCULATED FOR THE

Service both of LONDON and the COUNTRY;

And directing what is neceffary to be done in the *Providing for*, *Conducting*, and *Managing* a FAMILY throughout the Year.

CONTAINING

A general Account of frefh Provifions of all Kinds. Of the feveral *foreign Articles* for the Table, pickled, or otherwife preferved; and the different Kinds of *Spices*, *Salts*, *Sugars*, and other *Ingredients* ufed in *Pickling* and *Preferving* at Home : Shewing *what* each is, *whence* it is brought, and what are its *Qualities* and *Ufes*.

Together with the *Nature* of all Kinds of *Foods*, and the Method of *fuiting them to different* CONSTITUTIONS;

A BILL of FARE for each Month, the Art of *Marketing* and *chufing* frefh Provifions of all Kinds; and the making as well as chufing of Hams, *Tongues*, and other *Store Difhes*.

Alfo DIRECTIONS for plain *Roafting* and *Boiling*; and for the Dreffing of all Sorts of *Made Difhes* in various Taftes; and the preparing the *Defert* in all its Articles.

Containing a greater Variety than was ever before publifh'd, of the moft Elegant, yet leaft Expenfive RECEIPTS in

COOKERY,	FRICASSEES,	TARTS,	DRY'D FRUITS,
PASTRY,	RAGOUTS,	CAKES,	SWEETMEATS,
PUDDINGS,	SOUPS,	CREAMS,	MADE WINES,
PRESERVES,	SAUCES,	CUSTARDS,	CORDIALS, And
PICKLES,	JELLIES,	CANDIES,	DISTILLERY.

To which are annexed,

The Art of CARVING; and the Terms ufed for cutting up various Things ; and the polite and eafy Manner of *doing the Honours of the Table :* The whole Practice of *Pickling* and *Preferving :* And of preparing *made Wines*, *Beer*, and *Cyder*.

As alfo of *diftilling* all the ufeful Kinds of *Cordial* and *Simple* Waters.

With the *Conduct of a Family* in Refpect of *Health* ; the *Diforders* to which they are every *Month* liable, and the moft approved *Remedies* for each.

And a Variety of other valuable Particulars, neceffary to be known in *All Families*; and nothing inferted but what has been *approved* by EXPERIENCE.

Alfo the Ordering of all Kinds of profitable *Beafts* and *Fowls*, with refpect to their *Choice*, their *Breeding* and *Feeding* ; the *Difeafes* to which they are feverally liable each Month, and *Receipts* for their *Cure.* Together with the Management of the *pleafant*, *profitable*, and *ufeful Garden.*

THE WHOLE

Embellifhed with a great Number of *curious* COPPER PLATES, fhewing the Manner of *Truffing* all Kinds of GAME, wild and tame FOWLS, &c. as alfo the Order of fetting out TABLES for *Dinners*, *Suppers*, and *Grand Entertainments*, in a Method never before attempted ; and by which even *thofe who cannot read* will be able to inftruct themfelves.

By Mrs. MARTHA BRADLEY, *late of* BATH :
Being the Refult of upwards of *Thirty Years Experience.*

The whole (which is deduc'd from Practice) compleating the careful Reader, from the higheft to the loweft Degree, in every Article of *Englifh* Houfewifery.

L O N D O N :
Printed for *S. Crowder* and *H. Woodgate*, at the *Golden Ball* in *Paternofter Row.*

A Table for a Wedding Supper.

You may change all the outside Dishes with Sweetmeats or move the 8 small ones, &
let the plates stand according to pleasure.

THE
COOK, HOUSEKEEPER's,
AND
GARDINER's COMPANION.

✦✦✦✦✦✦✦✦✦✦✦✦✦✦✦✦✦✦✦✦✦✦✦✦✦✦✦✦✦✦✦✦✦✦✦✦✦

A P R I L.

✦✦✦✦✦✦✦✦✦✦✦✦✦✦✦✦✦✦✦✦✦✦✦✦✦✦✦✦✦✦✦✦✦✦✦✦✦

S E C T. I.

Of Marketing and Providing.

WE fhall here, as in the Beginning of each preceding Month, acquaint the careful Provider
what is in Seafon, and lay before her a Lift of Articles
out of which fhe is to furnifh her Table. The candid
Reader will pardon us if fome Things occur in this
Lift which were mentioned in the former. We chufe
Repetitions rather than Omiffions, and there are many
Difhes that continue from Month to Month for a confiderable Time, fome the whole Year.

This is not a Month of the greateft Choice, for many
of the Winter Articles are gone out, and very few of
the Summer ones are come in ; but we fhall fhew the
careful Provider that there is at every Seafon a Store
not only for fufficient Supply, but for great Variety.

A Bill of Fare for APRIL.

THE various Kinds from which we have directed
a Supply for the preceding Months are ftill
ready at Hand, and if fome of them fupply fewer, yet
there is in others an Encreafe that makes Amends.

ART.

ART. I. *Butchers Meat.*

This is a conftant and fure Refource. We lofe the Winter Fowl in Summer, and the Products of the Garden in general fail in Winter; but the Market is ftill filled with Flefh Meat. We have given a great many Methods of drefling it in its feveral Kinds, and fhall many more; for the Art of the Cook is no more confined than the Hand of Nature.

The Ox is at all Times brought to the Slaughter, and affords us a long Lift of Pieces. We have recommended the larger and more fubftantial of thefe in the Winter Months, but there are enough for this or they may be repeated. A boiled Rump is fitteft for Winter, but there is no Time when a Sirloin is not in Seafon. The feveral fmaller boiling Pieces may alfo be brought in now; and though we don't advife bringing the Rump whole to Table, the Larder fhould not be without it, for many nice fmall Difhes that we fhall name depend upon it.

Veal is very fine at this Seafon; the Neck boiled, or the Knuckle with a Ham, is fit for any Table. At large Entertainments a Chine of Veal makes a good Appearance, the Head is ufeful many Ways, the Fillet cut into Collops, and the Loin for Ragoos.

The Leg of Lamb with Spinage is very fit at this Time, and other Parts of it ftewed, forced, or ragoo'd, or in Pies.

As we fhall have from good Gardens fome of the early Summer Products, we fhall find Lamb very fit for them; any Part roafted introduces French Beans and Cucumbers in their young and nice State better than larger Joints or ftronger Meats. In a well-regulated Table thefe young Greens fhould have young Meats with them.

Hams yet are very proper with Pigeons, with Veal, or in the good old Way, with Chickens; but let them be fmall and young ones.

2. *Poultry.*

2. *Poultry.*

Pigeons are in high Seafon now, and there is no Time of the Year more favourable for Chickens ; they are young and delicate, and properly fatted up at this Seafon exceed any others. The Farmer's earlieft Breeds of them come in now, and bring a Price that pays him very well for the Charge and Trouble of raifing.

Green Geefe and Ducklings are alfo in high Seafon. Young Chickens and Afparagus is elegant, and the fine fmall Rabbits, which all the Markets afford at this time, anfwer in Fricaffees nearly as well as Chickens. Let not the critical Reader defpife us for placing Rabbits among the Poultry; we are informing the Houfekeeper what fhe will find at the Poulterers.

3. *Fish.*

Of the Fifh Kind there are feveral in Seafon ; toward the End of the Month Mackarel will come in, and young Goofeberries will be growing to a Bignefs for them. Smelts are fine this Month, and there are Herrings, Mullets, and feveral others.

Of the Shell-fifh Kind there are yet Oifters, but they are growing out of Seafon ; this is the laft Month for them till after Summer. Crabs and Lobfters are in very good Seafon now, and Prawns.

From the frefh Waters we have Carp, Tench, Pike, Pearch, and Gudgeons. Eels are alfo very good in this Month, better than in the Heat of Summer.

4. *Greens and Roots.*

Salleting is this Month in great Perfection, and there is Afparagus very fine.

There are Sprouts from Savoy and Cabbage-plants, and young Shoots of Brocoli very delicate. Coleworts are yet good, and there is Celeri, Beet, and Endive.

Lettuces begin to come in ; the Dutch brown, and common Cabbage are in good Order ; and there are fine young Cos-lettuces in the greateft Perfection.

The

The Shoots of the Hop-plant, called Hop-tops, are now in Perfection; and there is another Shoot not fo much known in England as it ought to be, this is the Salfify; our Markets afford fome of it, and it may always be raifed in the Garden of the Family; many prefer it to Afparagus; it is at leaft equal to that, and has the Advantage of Variety.

Some Peafe may very well be expected this Month in a good Garden, and the Markets afford them. There are alfo French Beans raifed on Hot-beds, and alfo Cucumbers, as we have mentioned already.

As to Roots there are many; Radifhes will now be in Perfection; Beet-root continues good, and there are Parfnips and Carrots. Thefe are not to be looked for in the Garden, for fuch as have ftood the Winter in the Ground have fhot by this time, and are fticky; but thofe kept in Sand are fine yet. There will alfo be young Carrots from the Autumn fowing for that Purpofe; thefe will yield a very fair Supply of Variety in this Article.

5. *Fruits.*

The Store of Fruits preferved through the Winter are now in a Manner gone, and but few of thofe which Art brings forward before their proper time are yet come in, but there are fome of each.

Apples and Pears are the only Kinds that can be expected to laft yet of the Stores of the former Year, and of thefe but a few Kinds; the John Apple and the Stone Pippin remain ftill, as alfo the Nonpareil; there are three of the Ruffets alfo which hold out yet; thefe are Pile's and Wheeler's, and the Golden Ruffet.

The two beft Pears at this time are the Bergamot Bugi, and the Carmelite; the Franc-Real and Saint Martial keep yet, as do alfo the Lord Cheyne's Winter Green and Chamontelle; thefe are for eating. Par-kinfon's Pear and the other Warden, commonly called the Englifh Warden, hold good for baking, and the Cardillac.

N°. XI.   R r   Thefe

Thefe are the Remains of the laft Year ; as to the forward Fruits of the prefent, they are owing to artificial Means, to forcing Frames and Dung ; but we have from the Hot-bed Strawberries, and from the Frames we have Apricots, that Kind called the Mafculine ; alfo Cherries, and fome of the early Plumbs ; thefe, whether raifed or purchafed, come fo dear that they are only for the Tables of the Great ; but they make a very agreeable Appearance there ; their Novelty gives them an additional Value, and they foretel Summer.

S E C T. II.

Cookery.

OUR Cook is by this time, from the plain and exact Directions laid down in our feveral preceding Numbers, prepared for the common Bufinefs of her Profeffion ; and, being well grounded in that, fhe will find it eafy to do all the reft to Satisfaction ; fhe will be able to fhew that an Englifh Girl, properly inftructed at firft, can equal the beft French Gentleman in every thing but Expence. It is only in the being better taught at firft, that thefe Foreigners excel our own People ; let them have the fame Advantages, and they may defy them. It is this we have endeavoured to give them in the prefent Book, and we hope we have hitherto fucceeded.

C H A P. I.

Of Roafting.

WE have given the full Directions for this Article in the common Joints, therefore the Englifh Cook has the Rudiments of her Profeffion in that Article. We fhall now fhew her the greater Extent and Elegance.   A R T.

ART. I. *To roaſt Veniſon the Italian Way.*

Put into a Bowl a good Quantity of ſweet Baſil cut
ſmall, with ſome Sprigs of Thyme, ſweet Marjoram,
and Winter Savoury; cut in ſome Chibols, and ſhred
ſome Parſley fine; ſprinkle in ſome Pepper and Salt,
and pour upon all this two Quarts of Vinegar.

Let theſe ſtand all Night, next Morning add half
an Ounce of Mace, ten Cloves, two Nutmegs broke
ſmall, and a Pinch of Saffron, ten Bay Leaves, and
a couple of chopt Onions; ſtir all up well together.

Cut ſome large and thick Pieces of Fat Bacon for
larding, lard the Haunch of Veniſon well with them,
ſtrew it over with ſome ſweet Herbs and Spices, the
ſame that are put in the Vinegar; and laſt of all with
a little Pepper. Lay it in a long deep Pan, pour the
Vinegar and Ingredients upon it, turn it once in twelve
Hours, and let it lie thus three Days, then ſpit it,
roaſt it carefully, and baſte it with the Pickle.

Send up with it ſome rich Gravy, with a good deal
of Pepper and a little Vinegar in it.

This is a famous Diſh with the Foreigners, but a
plain Haunch is preferable. It makes a Variety however, and as there are Palates it will pleaſe, 'tis fit the
Cook know how to do it; ſhe muſt be able to dreſs
Things not only the beſt Way, but the Way they will
be liked beſt.

A Turkey with Oiſters the French Way.

Pick and draw the Turkey, cut the Liver to Pieces,
and ſet it over the Fire in a Stewpan with twenty
Oiſters in their Liquor, ſome Pepper and Salt, a couple of Bay Leaves, and two Blades of Mace; add a
Piece of Butter rolled in Flour, and ten or a dozen
ſmall Muſhrooms. Set this over a very moderate
Fire, ſhake it once and cover it, then ſinge the Turkey, and as ſoon as this is done take off the Stewpan,
draw all the Ingredients together with a Spoon; if
they have been well heated thro' it is enough; ſtuff the

R r 2 　　　　　Turkey

Turkey with the whole Parcel, and then carefully ſpit it.

Cover it with broad thin Slices of Bacon, put a buttered Paper over theſe, and lay it down to a good Fire, but at a proper Diſtance.

While the Turkey is roaſting ſet on a Stewpan with half a Pint of Eſſence of Ham; throw a Pint of Oiſters into ſome boiling Water, this will blanch them, take them out, take off the Beards, throw them into the Eſſence of Ham, and add a little Juice of Lemon to give it a Tartneſs. Take Care this be hot when the Turkey is enough, and when that is laid in the Diſh pour this over it and ſend it up hot.

3. *A Quarter of Pig Lamb Faſhion.*

The former are roaſt Diſhes of ſome Expence, this and the following are more generally uſeful.

Let the hind Quarter of a large Pig be cut Lamb Faſhion, ſkin it, and ſtrew it over with ſhred Parſley, lay it down at a Diſtance, and by Degrees bring it nearer the Fire, ſo as to brown it up thoroughly at laſt.

Have ſome Mint Sauce made of very young Mint, chopped with Sugar and Vinegar, to ſerve up with it; and juſt as it is going to Table ſqueeze over it a very little Juice of a fine Seville Orange .

It makes a very pleaſant Diſh, and the Company are often confounded what to make of it; but they many Times take it for Lamb, and thoſe who think otherwiſe ſay it is like Houſe Lamb, but better. It is a Diſh always approved.

4. *A Fowl Pheaſant Faſhion.*

Chuſe a fine large grown Fowl, keep the Head on, and truſs it as a Pheaſant, lard it with thin Slips of Bacon, and roaſt it carefully at a Diſtance firſt, and afterwards near. Send it up with the ſame Sauce that is is uſed for Pheaſants, which we have named before, and many People will be deceived: Thoſe that are not will be very well pleaſed with it, for a Fowl no other Way eats ſo well.

If

If there be one Pheafant roafted plain, and a Fowl thus larded Pheafant-fafhion, fent up in a Difh to- gether, the Gravy mixing and going with them, few will know the Difference. I have feen in fuch a Cafe the Fowl preferred to the Pheafant by all the Company.

5. *Teal with Olives.*

Pick and draw the Teal, cut the Livers to Pieces, mix with them fome fweet Herbs picked from the Stalks, an Onion cut fine, fome Pepper and Salt, half a Blade of Mace, half a dozen Mufhrooms, and a good Piece of Bacon ; all thefe Ingredients are to be minced fine together, and the Bodies of the Teal ftuffed with them ; then they are to be laid down to roaft, covered with broad thin Slices of Bacon, and with buttered Paper over them.

While the Teal are roafting, the Sauce is to be made thus :

Chufe fome large fine Olives, clear the flefhy Part from the Stones, and put it into fome Veal Gravy.

Set on a Stewpan with a quarter of a Pint of Effence of Ham ; when it is hot put in the Veal Gravy and the Olives ; let them once boil up.

When the Teal are enough lay them in a Difh, and pour this rich and elegant Sauce over them.

6. *A Green Goofe with Chefnuts.*

Draw and pick a well-grown Green Goofe, finge it carefully, and lay it ready on the Dreffer. While the Goofe is preparing let there be fome Chefnuts laid to roaft in the Embers or among the Cinders ; when they are fo done that the hard Skin will fepa- rate, take that off, and lay them in again ; when they are well heated through again, fkin them a fecond Time to make them perfectly clean.

Then cut to Pieces the Liver of the Goofe, with a good Slice of fat Bacon, cut alfo very fmall, a dozen Mufhrooms, and four or five Morells ; flice two Truffles,

Truffles, and add fome fweet Herbs, Pepper, Salt, and a Blade of Mace beaten to Pieces; put all thefe into a Stewpan with a Piece of Butter, cover them up, fet them on a moderate Fire, and let them be well heated through.

Put this into the Body of the Goofe, and put along in this three good Saufages pricked all over; when the Stuffing is all in lay the Goofe down to roaft.

While the Goofe is roafting put fome more Chefnuts to do in the Cinders, and when they are thoroughly done, and well peeled, fet on a Stewpan with fome Beef Gravy; let the Chefnuts be bruifed in a Mortar and put into the Gravy, and ftewed till they are perfectly foft. When the Goofe is enough lay it in a Difh, and pour the Sauce over it. Some make the Sauce richer, but this is better.

C H A P. II.

Of Boiling.

AS we have led the Cook in the Article of roafting from the plaineft to fome of the moft elegant Difhes prepared by that Kind of Cookery, we fhall do the fame in Refpect to boiling in the following Chapters.

A R T. I. *Salmon boiled in Wine.*

Chufe a fine prime Piece of frefh Salmon when in the higheft Seafon, fcale it, wafh it carefully, and lay it ready; cut fome Slices of Bacon, Fat and Lean together, cut a Pound of Veal thin, and a Pound and half of Beef; ftrew in fome Pepper and Salt over thefe, and put them into a deep Stewpan, put the Salmon upon them, and pour in as much Water as will juft cover it, and no more; fet it over a gentle Fire, and let it fcimmer till the Salmon is near done.

Then

Then drain away all the Water pretty clofe, pour in two Quarts of ftrong white Wine, and put in at the fame Time an Onion cut to Pieces, and fome Thyme and fweet Marjoram ftripped from the Stalks ; let it ftew gently again, and while this is doing cut a Sweetbread into thin Slices, cut it again croffwife, and fet it to ftew in a Saucepan with fome rich Veal Gravy ; when it is done enough add a quarter of a Pint of Effence of Ham ; take up the Salmon, lay it in a Difh, and pour the Sauce over it. Serve it up very hot.

2. *Boiled Soals the Dutch Way.*

Chufe a Pair of large Soals, gut them, and take off the Skin, then wafh them very clean in cold Spring Water.

Set on a Stewpan with fome Water and a little Salt, when it boils put in the Soals, and let them boil a few Minutes.

Set on a fmall Stewpan with fome chopped Parfley in a little Water, let it ftand till the Water is almoft all confumed, then duft in fome Flour, and put in a good Piece of Butter ; fhake this together till all is well mixed, and then lay the Soals, carefully drained, upon a Difh, and pour this Sauce over them.

This is a very plain Way of dreffing Soals, but they have the full fine Flavour ; and to thofe who are fond of the real Tafte of the Fifh, this is preferable to any other Way.

3. *Boiled Soals with white Wine.*

Chufe three Pair of middling Soals, fcale them, gut them, and wafh them clean in cold Spring Water ; when taken out of that lay them on a Difh, and pour half a Pint of white Wine over them ; turn them once or twice in it, then pour it away.

Cut off the Heads, Tails, and Fins of the Soals thus cleaned and feafoned with the Wine, and fet them ready. Set on a Stewpan with a little rich Fifh Broth, put in an Onion cut to Pieces, a Bundle of
fweet

fweet Herbs, fome Pepper, Salt, and a Blade of Mace; when this boils up put in the Soals, and with them half a Lemon cut into Slices, Peel and all; let them be well heated, then take out the fweet Herbs, and pour in a Pint of ftrong white Wine; at the fame Time put in a Lump of Butter rolled in Flour; let all boil up together to mix well, and finifh the doing of the Soals.

While this is doing, mix in a Saucepan half a Pint of Veal Gravy, and a quarter of a Pint of Effence of Ham; take up the Soals, and pour this over them.

4. *To boil French Beans.*

French Beans being juft coming into Seafon, we fhall lay down the Method of dreffing them : Nothing is eafier; but as we had not Occafion to mention them in the preceding Months among the plain and common Receipts, that nothing may be wanting we fhall give the Method here.

Cut off the Stalk End, and, beginning at the other, ftring them carefully. The Strings are very tender at this early Seafon, and for that Reafon fome may think there is no great need of Care in this Article, for if they break, and a Part be left on, 'tis, as they think, no great Matter; but the good Cook will think juft otherwife; the Strings are as hard in Proportion to the Beans now as they are in the Seafon when they are larger: The Beans never are fo delicate as now, and nothing is fo proper as to fend them up accordingly; a careful Hand muft therefore be employed, and they muft be made perfectly free from the Strings, Stalks, and Tips.

Let a Bowl of Spring Water and a little Bafket Salt diffolved in it ftand at your Elbow, and as the Beans are cleaned and ftringed throw them in.

When all are done fet on a fmall Stewpan for boiling of them, and put fome Salt into the Water; fee the Pan and the Water be perfectly clean, let the Fire be be clear, and when the Water boils put in the Beans; when they have boiled a little while take one out and taſte it; as ſoon as they are tender throw them into a Cullander, and in the mean Time melt ſome Butter very thick and fine; lay the Beans on a Plate in a little Heap, higheſt in the Middle, and ſend up the Butter in a Sauce-boat.

This is the French Way, for they ſend up the Beans whole, which is much the beſt Method when they are thus young, and being whole they better pre-ſerve their delicate green Colour.

When a little more grown they muſt be cut a-croſs in two after ſtringing; and for common Tables, when older, they are to be ſplit firſt, and cut a-croſs afterwards; but thoſe who are nice never have them at ſuch a Growth as to require ſplitting.

5. *Boiled ſalt Cod the Italian Way.*

Chuſe a fine Piece, and lay it to ſoak in a great deal of Water; when it is ſoaked, clean it tho-roughly, and ſet it on in a large Stewpan, with a great deal of very clean Water; let it boil up once or twice, then ſet it off.

Set on another Stewpan with a good Piece of But-ter, put to this a Handful of young Onions cut very ſmall, a good Handful of Parſley cut ſmall, two Cloves of Garlick ſhred, and ſome Thyme and Sweet Marjoram Leaves picked clean from the Stalks; when theſe are warm together, take out the Cod from the Water in the other Stewpan and lay it into this upon theſe Ingredients; ſqueeze a large Seville Orange Orange over it, duſt on a little Pepper, and pour in half a Gill of ſweet and fine Oil; ſet all over the Fire, ſtir it frequently about, turn it two or three Times, and taſte it to find whether it be well reliſhed, if not, add more Pepper or more Orange Juice; then diſh it up hot, and ſend up with it Gravy, with Eſ-ſence of Ham for thoſe who chuſe it.

N°. XI. S ſ C H A P.

C H A P. III.

Of Broiling.

IN this, as in the foregoing Chapters, we fhall lead the Cook, who underftands the Rudiments of her Profeffion, to fome very elegant Difhes, moft of them at a very moderate Expence, therefore generally ufeful.

A R T. I. *To broil Eels.*

Chufe Eels of a moderate Size, thofe of about three quarters of a Pound Weight are fitteft for this Purpofe; take off the Skin, cut them into Pieces as long as one's Finger, and with a fharp-pointed Knife cut Slafhes in them length-ways in feveral Places.

Set on a Saucepan with fome Butter to melt in the ufual Way, when it is melted ftrew in fome Pepper and Salt, fome Leaves of Thyme, and Pot Marjoram ftripped clean from the Stalks, an Onion cut to Pieces, and fome Parfley; fhake thefe well together, and then put in the Pieces of Eel; fhake them about a Minute or two over the Fire, then take them off, and pour all into a Bafon.

Rub a Quantity of Crumb of Bread to fine Powder between two Cloths, fet a Gridiron high over a very clear Fire, lay thefe Crumbs upon a Dreffer, take out the Eel Piece by Piece, and roll them in the Bread till well covered with it; then lay them on and broil them to a fine crifp brown.

While the Eels are dreffing fet on fome Veal Gravy in a fmall Saucepan, and add to it fome Chives cut very fine, fome Parfley fhred fine, and fome Capers, with the Flefh of half a dozen Olives; fhake them about for fome Minutes that all may be well heated together, and then take off the Eels; pour this Sauce into a Difh, and lay the Eels in it.

2. *To broil Salmon.*

Chufe fome fine frefh Salmon cut into proper Pieces, and wipe them clean and dry; melt fome Butter very rich, with a little Flour and a fprinkling of Bafket Salt; put the Pieces of Salmon into this, and roll them about that they may be very well covered with it all over; then lay them on a clean Gridiron, and broil them over a flack Fire.

While the Salmon is broiling let the Sauce be made for it thus.

Wafh a couple of Anchovies and take out the Bones, cut them into fmall Pieces, and cut a Leek into three or four long Pieces; fet on a Saucepan with fome Butter and a Duft of Flour, put in thefe Ingredients, and alfo fome Capers cut fmall, fome Pepper, Salt, and a little Nutmeg; add a little warm Water, and two Spoonfuls of Vinegar; melt the Butter, and fhake all together.

When the Salmon is done on one Side turn it on the other, and when it is enough take it off; then take the Leek out of the Sauce, and pour the reft into the Difh; add a little Orange-juice, then lay in the broiled Pieces of Salmon in a regular Manner.

CHAP. IV.

Of Frying.

WE have fhewn the common Ufe of frying, in Steaks and the like, but we fhall now lay before the Cook feveral other Articles, in which that Sort of Cookery may be employed in a much more elegant Manner.

ART. I. *Fried Eels.*

Skin and gut the Eels, and then take out the Bone; the larger Eels are, for frying in this Way, the better.

When

When they are thus cleaned and prepared, cut them in Pieces as long as a Finger.

Put into a Soup Dish a Quart of Vinegar, strew in some Pepper and Salt, put in five Bay Leaves cut into two or three Pieces; add two Onions cut in Pieces, and some Juice of Lemon. Lay the Eels, boned and and cut to Pieces, in this Pickle for three Hours, turning them carefully several Times.

Take them out, drudge them well with Flour, set on a Stewpan with clarified Butter, and fry them brown. Fry some Parsley and serve it up with them dry. Some chuse Gravy Sauce to them.

2. *Fried Salt Fish.*

Chuse a fine Piece of salt Cod, water it well, and when it is perfectly fresh cut it into Slices. Set on a Pan with some clarified Butter, dry the salt Fish carefully, then drudge it with Flour, and when it is well covered in every Part put it into the Pan of Butter, fry it brown, and send it up hot with fried Parsley. Any other Sauce may be sent up with it, according to the Pleasure of the Mistress.

3. *Fried Mushrooms.*

Pick and skin a Quantity of Mushrooms of a middling Growth, when very small and round they are called Buttons, and when full grown and spread they are called Flaps. Neither of these are fit, but such as are of the Breadth of a Crown-piece or somewhat more, and are neither flat nor round, but hollow. These are the proper Mushrooms for frying, and they make a Dish whereof many are very fond. These are to be cleaned and prepared by skinning, and when in this Order they are to be put into a Saucepan with a a little Veal Gravy and a few Corns of whole Pepper; set them on the Fire and shake them about a little. All that is meant by this is to deaden their Stiffness, and to give them a little Relish. When they fall, pour them into a Cullander and let the Gravy drain off, but

but fave it, for it is better than it was before for any
Ufe; the Mufhrooms have given it as much Tafte as
they have taken from it at leaft.

When the Mufhrooms are drained pour them out
upon a Cloth; fprinkle them over with Pepper and
Salt, then drudge a very fmall Quantity of Flour over
them, and fry them in Butter till they are enough.
Send them up with fried Parfley, and fend up fome
rich Beef Gravy in a Sauce-boat for fuch as like it.

4. *Fried Morels.*

Set fome Mutton Gravy over the Fire in a Saucepan, clean fome frefh Morels perfectly, and cut them
into thick Slices and throw them into the Gravy with
a Blade of Mace and four or five whole Cloves; let
them boil up once, then ftrain off the Liquor, pour
out the Morels on a Cloth and drudge them with
Flour. Save the Gravy, fet on a Stewpan with Butter,
fry the Morels after well drudging them with Flour,
and ferve them up with the Gravy thickened, by Way
of Sauce.

The Reader will be pleafed to obferve we have here
faid frefh Morels. This Method will not do for fuch
as are fold dry. We have explained the Nature of the
Morel in our firft Month, to which we refer.

5. *Fried Beet-Root.*

Chufe fome large and fine Beet-roots, and fend them
in a Pan to an Oven to be baked, or they may in
London be bought ready baked at the French Sallad
Shops and Cellars.

Peel the Roots when baked, and cut them into long
Slices: They muft not be cut croffwife, but fplit down
into Pieces of half an Inch thick; each good Root into
three or four Slices.

When thefe Slices are cut, make a rich Batter for
them thus.

Break half a dozen Eggs, take all the Yolks and
three of the Whites, beat thefe up, grate in fome Nutmeg, fprinkle in a little Pepper and Salt; add four

Cloves

Cloves bruised to Powder; beat all up, then put in a Quarter of a Pint of Cream, and the same Quantity of Mountain Wine. When all these are well mixed, bring in as much fine Flour as will make them into Batter, and then throw in the Slices of Beet.

Shred some Parsley very fine, rub some Bread to Crumb, and mix these and a little Flour.

When the Slices of Beet are well covered with the Batter, take them out, drudge them over with this Mixture, and fry them in Butter; serve them up hot, and squeeze over them some Juice of Seville Orange just as they go up.

C H A P. V.

Of Baking.

WE shall add two to the former Articles of this Kind in the present Number; one very elegant, and the other, though but coarse in Name, yet, when well done, an excellent Dish, and esteemed by many.

A R T. I. *Baked Ox Cheek.*

Clean an Ox Cheek perfectly well, and put it into a coarse strong earthen Pan that will hold it, with some Room for other Ingredients: Stick two large Onions with Cloves, a dozen in each Onion, put these into the Pan; then put a large Bundle of sweet Herbs, two Carrots cut in long Slices, four Blades of Mace, some Pepper and Salt, a Handful of Champignons, or wild Mushrooms, and two Quarts of Porter; shake all these well together, and then pour in as much Water as will cover all up.

Butter well a couple of Sheets of Cartouch Paper, and tie them fast over the Pan, one after the other. Let it be thoroughly well done.

When it comes home pour a good Quantity of the Gravy into a Saucepan, add to it a Gill of red

Port

Port Wine, and a large Piece of Butter rolled in Flour.

Thicken this up, and then take out the Head, lay it in a very large Diſh, and pour this excellent Gravy over it. It is very rich and fine.

2. *Baked Muſhrooms.*

Lay at the Bottom of a ſmall China Tart-pan a couple of Slices of very fine fat Bacon, ſprinkle over this ſome ſhred Parſley, and ſtrew on a little Pepper; then lay in a good Quantity of middle-ſized Muſhrooms, ſuch as we directed to be uſed for frying; let them be well picked and ſkinned; ſprinkle among theſe ſome Pepper and Salt; lay here and there among them a few Shalots, then lay over them two or three more Slices of Bacon cut very thin, and ſtrew upon this a Blade of Mace bruiſed to Powder, and a little Pepper.

Tie a Piece of double Cartouch Paper over the Pan, buttered between the Doublings, and thus ſend it to the Oven. It will come home a rich and fine Diſh.

C H A P. VI.

Of Sauces.

WE have laid down the Rudiments of Cookery, and we now come to the Practice of the Art in its full Perfection: The Cook knows already how to make the ordinary Sauces, ſhe will here ſee how ſhe is to anſwer the Demand at the moſt elegant Tables, and that without the great Expence which muſt be when made according to the Sauce Receipts in the uſual Books of Cookery. It is in this Article the French excel us principally: The Cooks of that Nation have beggared many great Families, but we propoſe in this Book to introduce all the Elegance of their Diſhes at a moderate Price.

A R T.

ART. I. *Ham Sauce.*

When a Ham is pretty well eaten down, fo that it cannot appear again at Table, nor any handfome Slices be cut from it, pick all the Meat clear from the Bone, beat this well with a Rolling-pin that it may be broke in every Part ; put this Mafh into a Saucepan, and pour in about three Spoonfuls of any common Gravy.

Set it over a fmall Fire, cover it, and ftir it about till it fticks to the Bottom of the Saucepan ; then drudge in a little Flour, and keep ftirring it about for fome Time, for it will more and more ftick to the Bottom.

After fome Time pour in half a Pint of Beef Gravy, and at the fame Time add a fmall Bundle of fweet Herbs and fome Pepper ; cover it up, and let it ftew over a gentle Fire : When it is thoroughly done ftrain off the Gravy.

This is an excellent Sauce for Veal, Capons, or common Fowls, and may be feafoned higher at Pleafure.

2. *Orange Sauce for Ducks.*

Put into a Saucepan a quarter of a Pint of Veal Gravy and half a Gill of Port Wine, fet it over the Fire, and let it once boil up ; then fqueeze in the Juice of two Seville Oranges and one Lemon ; fet it on again to be hot, duft in a little Pepper, and then pour it hot into the Difh.

It is fit for Wild Duck, Teal, Widgeon, and all the Water Fowl of the wild Kind whatfoever.

3. *Green Sauce for Lamb.*

Cut a Handful of young green Wheat, put it into a Marble Mortar, with a fmall Cruft of Bread, pound them thoroughly together, and add a little Pepper and Salt ; put in after this a Spoonful of Vinegar and four Spoonfuls of Veal Gravy ; grind all together, and then ftrain the Liquor through a Sieve, and fend

up

up in a Sauce-boat. Nothing gives fo fine a green as young Wheat.

4. *Woodcock Sauce.*

When the Woodcocks are roafted take out the Guts and the Livers, bruife them with a Spoon to a Mafh, and fprinkle on them a little Pepper and Salt; add two Spoonfuls of red Port, and a fmall Piece of Butter rolled in Flour; boil all up together.

The Way of fending up this is to pour it hot into a Difh, and cut up the Woodcocks in it, fo fending them to Table.

5. *Shalot Sauce.*

Set on fome Veal Gravy in a fmall Saucepan, peel fome Shalots, and cut them very fine and fmall, ftrew Pepper and Salt upon them, and fpread them over the Bottom of the Difh; when the Gravy is hot pour it upon them, and immediately after lay in the Meat.

This is very good with roaft Mutton, and many are fond of it with roafted Fowls, Chickens, or Capons.

6. *Rich Caper Sauce.*

Drain fome Capers from their Liquor and cut them fmall; put into a fmall Saucepan fome Effence of Ham, fprinkle in a little Pepper, and let it boil up; then put in the Capers; let it boil up again two or three Times, then ferve it up hot.

Our Way is to mix Capers with melted Butter; but whoever has once tafted the French Caper Sauce will have no Relifh for the greafy Kind in common Ufe.

To fave the Expence of Effence of Ham, our common Ham Sauce will do.

7. *Onion Sauce, the French Way.*

Set on a Saucepan with half a Pint of Veal Gravy, cut to Pieces three good Onions, mincing them very

N°. XI. T t fine,

fine, ſtrew a little Pepper and Salt over them, and then put them into the Gravy; let them ſcimmer gently till the Onions begin to be tender, and then ſtrain off the clear Gravy.

8. *Sweet Sauce.*

Bruiſe a good Stick of Cinnamon, ſet it over the Fire in a Saucepan with juſt as much Water as will cover it, boil it up two or three Times, then put in a couple of Spoonfuls of the fineſt Sugar beaten to Powder, and a quarter of a Pint of white Wine, break in two Bay Leaves, boil all up together, and then ſtrain it through a Sieve, and ſend it up hot in a Sauce-boat. It ſerves many Things.

9. *Gooſberry Sauce for Mackarel.*

Melt a little Butter in a Saucepan, add a Duſt of Flour, brown it, and then throw in ſome Chives minced very fine.

When theſe have been heated together add ſome Fiſh Gravy, and throw in ſome Bay Salt and a little Pepper.

Boil this up, and then put in two or three Sprigs of young Fennel, and ſome ſmall picked Gooſberries; keep it ſcimmering till the Gooſberries are tender, and then ſerve it up together.

We ſee in this, as in Caper Sauce, a great Difference between the French Method and the Engliſh, but the French is greatly preferable: We learnt ours of the Dutch, who butter every Thing.

10. *Sauce Robert.*

Cut ſome large Onions into Dice, or ſmall ſquare Pieces, but not ſo ſmall as by mincing, cut ſome fat Bacon in the ſame Manner, and put both together into a Saucepan, ſet them over the Fire, and keep them continually ſtirring about.

When they begin to be brown pour off the Fat, and pour in ſome rich Veal Gravy, add a little Pepper and Salt, and let them boil gently together

till

till the Onions are tender; then put in a little Muſtard and ſome Vinegar, and ſerve it up hot.

This is excellent with roaſt Pork, and it eats very well with a roaſt Gooſe, and many other Things.

C H A P. VII.

Of Culliſſes.

THESE are a particular Article of the French Cookery, which we have not named in the preceding Months, becauſe Victuals may be dreſſed in a plain Way very well without them; but they are eſſential to Made Diſhes, and will be found very uſeful on many other Occaſions; they are Things that ſhould be kept in the Houſe ready for different Purpoſes.

If any of the Sauces deſcribed in the laſt Chapter are too thin, a little Cullis of the proper Sort thickens them up; and in general it is an Addition to any of them to add Cullis, more or leſs, according to their Conſiſtence.

They are uſeful in the ſame Way in all Raggoos and in Soups, and as there are many Kinds of theſe, there are in the ſame Manner Culliſſes of the ſame Variety and Sorts for them.

This being ſufficient to explain the Nature of Culliſſes in general, and their Uſe, we ſhall proceed to give the ſeveral Kinds; and it will be the more proper to introduce them here, becauſe in the next Chapter we ſhall treat of ſome of the rich Soups, in which theſe are very proper Ingredients, as well as in the ſucceeding Made Diſhes.

A R T. I. *Cullis for Fleſh Soups.*

Chuſe a ſmall Piece of fine Sirloin of Beef, about ·five Pounds will be ſufficient, cut off all the Fat, and then roaſt the Meat very brown.

While

While this is roafting grate fome Crufts of Bread to a coarfe Powder.

When the Meat is done put it hot from the Spit into a large Marble Mortar, add the grated Bread, and beat all together to a Mafh; when it is beat well to Pieces pour in a little ftrong Beef Gravy, and work it well together, then put it into a Saucepan, add a little more Gravy, and tofs it in, feafoning it with Salt and Pepper, and with fome Slices of Lemon, Peel and all; let it boil together two or three Minutes, and then pafs it through a coarfe Hair Sieve, and fet it by for Ufe.

2. *Brown Cullis for Sauces.*

Cut three Pounds of a Fillet of Veal into thin Slices, cut out in the fame Manner three quarters of a Pound of the lean Part of a Gammon of Bacon; warm a Stewpan, and cover the Bottom of it with this Mixture of Veal and Bacon; cut into Slices fome Carrots, Parfnips, and Onions, throw thefe carelefsly over the Meat, cover up the Stewpan, and fet it on a very flow Fire.

When it begins to ftick to the Pan, and is well browned, add fome fat Bacon cut very fmall, and drudge on a very little Flour.

This done let it ftand a little longer, and then pour in fome Veal Gravy, let it boil up, then put in fome dried Mufhrooms, fome Truffles, and fome Morels, fome fhred Parfley, half a dozen Cloves, and a whole Leek; when it has fcimmered a quarter of an Hour put in fome Crufts of Bread, and when it has ftood fome Time ftrain it off.

While this is doing let a full-grown Fowl be roafted, and when well browned put it hot into a Marble Mortar with fome grated Crufts of Bread, and then pound it to Mafh; pour in the ftrained Liquor, and, when all is well mixed, put it into a Saucepan and boil it up; then ftrain it through a Sieve for Ufe.

3. *A*

3. *A Turkey Cullis.*

Lay down a large Turkey, roaft it till it be enough, and take Care it be thoroughly brown, then put it into a Marble Mortar, and pound it to Pieces; throw in fome broken Crufts of Bread, and fome Pieces of fat Bacon cut fmall; when all thefe are reduced to a Mafh, pour in fome Gravy of Veal; heat it well again.

Shred fome fweet Bafil and fome Parfley very fine, cut fome Mufhrooms very fmall, and mince fome Chives; throw thefe into the Mortar alfo, and mix all well together; then put it all into a deep Stewpan, cover it, and fet it over a Stove for a few Minutes; after this take off the Cover, and turn it two or three Times as it heats; then pour in a Quart of Veal Gravy, mix all well together, pour it into a coarfe Hair Sieve, and ftrain it off for Ufe.

4. *Fifh Cullis.*

Chufe a large Pike for this Purpofe, gut it, and lay it whole upon a Gridiron, turn it at Times, and when it is well done take it off, pull off the Skin, and feparate the Flefh from the Bones.

Boil half a dozen Eggs hard, take out the Yolks, and put them by in Readinefs.

Blanch a Handful of Almonds. When Things are thus ready put the Almonds into a Marble Mortar, and beat them to a Pafte; then add the Yolks of the Eggs, mix thefe well together, and then add the Fifh; beat all up to a Mafh.

Cut into thin Slices half a dozen Onions, a couple of Parfnips, and three Carrots, fet on a Stewpan with thefe Roots and fome Butter, turn them from Time to Time till they are brown, and then pour in a little Pea Broth to moiften it; when this has boiled up fome Time ftrain it off into another Stewpan, and put in a whole Leek, fome Parfley and fweet Bafil, half a dozen Cloves, fome Mufhrooms and Truffles,

and

and a Handful of Crumbs of Bread ; let this fcimmer
together a quarter of an Hour, and then mix in the
Fifh out of the Mortar; let it continue fcimmering
fome Time longer; it muft not boil up, for that
would make it brown; and when it is enough ftrain
it through a coarfe Hair Sieve.

It ferves to thicken up all Made Difhes and Soups
of Fifh for Lent.

5. *Cullis of Roots.*

Cut into fmall Pieces a good Quantity of Roots
of Parfley, and the fame Quantity of Carrots, Parfnips, and Onions; tofs them up a little in a Stewpan, when they are hot put them into a Marble Mortar, and pound them thoroughly till they are a Pap :
While thefe are pounding cut off the Cruft of two
French Rolls, and fet the Crumb to foak in fome rich
Fifh Broth ; blanch twenty Almonds, and put thefe
and the foaked Crumb of Bread into the Mortar to
the Roots; when all is well bruifed and mixed together by good beating, boil it all in a Saucepan with
a little Fifh Broth, and then ftrain it through a Sieve
as the other Culliffes, and feafon it well with Pepper
and Salt.

This ferves excellently for all Soups and Made
Difhes without Meat; it is very ufeful in Lent, and
nothing is more handy.

Thefe Culliffes are a Sort of Effence of the Ingredients, or they anfwer to what Chemifts and Apothecaries
call Extracts of Medicines; they contain all the
Virtues of the Ingredients in a fmall Compafs, and
are ready for mixing up with any Thing : They are
not expenfive nor very troublefome. The French
make them expenfive by adding Partridges and other
Birds of that Kind to their Meat Culliffes, and Carp
and fuch other Fifh to their Fifh Culliffes ; but thefe
we have named anfwer the Purpofe full as well, without
that great Expence.

When

When a Partridge Soup is made, as is common with them, and as we fhall fhew how hereafter, then it will be very proper to add a Partridge to the Cullis to give the Soup the more Flavour, and fo of other Kinds ; but excepting for thefe Ufes, for which we fhall feldom want them, the feveral Sorts may be made perfectly good according to thefe Directions.

6. *Cullis of Cray-fifh.*

Chufe a good Parcel of the largeft Cray-fifh, wafh them in feveral Waters, and then boil them ; when they are enough throw them into a Sieve to drain, pick the Flefh from the Shells, and lay that in one Difh and the Shells upon another.

Blanch a dozen and half of Almonds, beat them to a Pafte in a Marble Mortar, and then put in the Shells of the Cray-fifh ; pound thefe well together.

While they are pounding together cut an Onion into thin Slices, cut to Pieces in the fame Manner three Carrots and two large Parfnips, fet on a Stew-pan with a little Butter, throw in thefe Roots, and tofs them up till they begin to be brown, then pour on them fome Fifh Broth, and feafon with Pepper and Salt ; put in half a dozen Cloves bruifed, and fome Leaves of fweet Bafil : This is an Herb the French are very fond of, and we are not fo well acquainted with, but it gives an excellent Flavour to any Thing.

Let this fcimmer together, then add a whole Leek, fome Truffles, a Handful of Mufhrooms, fome Crufts of Bread, and fome fhred Parfley ; keep it hot over the Fire a quarter of an Hour, fcimmering all the Time, but not boiling up ; when it has been thus long hot put in the powdered Almonds and Cray-fifh Shells, and then boil it up heartily ; after it has boiled fome Time ftrain it through a Sieve, and keep it for Ufe.

The

The Flesh of the Cray-fishes serves for many other Purposes, as we shall shew in the succeeding Chapters. In this Case the Ligaments and Skins that remain about the Shells give the Cullis a sufficient Strength and Flavour. This Cullis has all the Advantage of those made only of Roots, and this rich Flavour from the Cray-fish beside.

Having in this Place given Directions for the making of so many Sorts of Culliffes, we may now proceed to the finer and more elegant Kinds of Soups, in which they are needful Additions; but we shall endeavour to reduce the Expence of many of these, so as to bring them within the Reach of a moderate Family, at the same time preserving all that is valuable in their Taste or Qualities. This is one of the chief Things we shall endeavour throughout the present Work, and we shall deliver nothing in it on this, or any other Head, but what the Mistress and the Cook may equally depend upon; nothing being set down but what have been frequently done for my Company, and the Receipts printed from the exact Copies of my own.

C H A P. VIII.

Of Soups.

A R T. I. *Soup de Santè.*

BUY a dozen Pounds of Beef, a fine Knuckle of Veal, and a large Fowl; set on the Beef in a Pot with as much Water as will cover it, and a couple of Quarts over; season it with Pepper, Salt, Spices, and a few sweet Herbs, boil it heartily, and when the Meat is very tender and the Broth is very strong, take it off the Fire.

Put into another Pot the Knuckle of Veal and the Fowl, strain off the Broth from the Beef into this Pot, and set it on to boil again, adding one Nutmeg
whole,

whole, and two or three Blades of Mace; boil this well, and the Liquor will be of the Strength of a Jelly with the rich Flavour of the Meat in it. When it is thus rich put in a large Slice of Bacon ftuck with a dozen Cloves, boil it up five Minutes longer, and then fet it off the Fire. This is the Broth for Soup de Sante.

The next Thing to be made is the Gravy which is to be done thus. Cut into thin Slices a quarter of a Pound of Bacon, lay it at the Bottom of a Stewpan, and put a Piece of Butter into it. Over this lay five Pounds of Veal cut into thin Slices, fet this over a clear Fire, and let it ftand a confiderable Time to colour. When it cracks put in fome of the Fat taken from the hot Broth, and ftir it very little. Cut to Slices a couple of Carrots, three Turnips, and one large Onion; throw thefe in, and with them fome Parfley fhred, fome Thyme Leaves ftripped from the Stalks, fome whole Pepper, and a few frefh Mufhrooms. Let all this be fried well together, and when it is of a good Colour put it all into the Pot of Broth which has been ftrained off from the Veal and Fowl. A little of this Broth muft left to keep the Veal and Fowl white, and to foften the Bread for the Soup.

When all is thus far ready cut to Pieces fome Endive and Dutch Lettuce, and with them fome Chervil and Celeri, when they are fmall, put them into a Saucepan, and pour fome of the Soup upon them, ftew them down with this, and then put in the Bread thus. Cut off the Crufts of two French Rolls, boil them up in three Pints of Gravy, and ftrain it thro' a Sieve; put this to the Herbs that are ftewing; when this has boiled up with the Herbs pour all together into the Pot with the reft, and let it boil a quarter of an Hour together, fkimming off the Fat at Times. The Soup is now finifhed, and will be exceeding fine, and it is to be ferved up thus.

Lay in the Bottom of a large Difh fome French Bread in Slices, or the Crufts of Rolls dried well before the Fire; either of thefe may be ufed according to Fancy, but whichever it is, it muft be foaked well in fome of the Broth left for that Purpofe in the firft Pot; and if it be the Crufts, they muft be boiled up in it to make them tender.

Thefe being laid in the Difh the Fowl is to be taken out of the Pot and laid in the Middle upon them, and the Herbs all about them, and then pour in the Soup. Garnifh it with boiled Celeri and Carrot.

This is an exceeding rich and fine Soup; the Quantity we have named is fit for the largeft Table, and if in a fmall Family it will ferve many Times, and will be every Time better and better.

The Receipt is long, but it is worth the Cook's while to underftand it well; for when fhe does, fhe will have the whole Art of making Soups, every thing being in a manner comprifed in this capital and general Article.

2. *Milk Soup.*

Set on two Quarts of new Milk in a Stewpan, and put into it two Sticks of Cinnamon, a couple of Bay-leaves, and a little Bafket Salt; add fome Sugar according to your Tafte, but don't let it be too much, for if this Soup be too fweet it is fpoiled.

Blanch half a Pound of fweet Almonds, and while the Milk is heating beat them up to a Pafte in a Marble Mortar, mix with them by Degrees a little Milk as they are beating, and by Degrees introduce more; bruife and fqueeze an unripe Lemon over the Almonds that the Zeft, or fine high Flavour of the Peel, may get in among the Almonds; then ftrain all this thro' a Sieve, and mix it with the Milk that is heating in the Stewpan; ftir all together well, and let it boil up.

Cut fome thin Slices of French Bread, and dry them before the Fire; then foak them a little in the Milk, and lay them in the Bottom of a Soup-difh, pour in the Soup, and garnifh it with fome broken Bifcuits; it is very rich and nourifhing.

3. *Hop-*

3. *Hop-top Soup.*

Cut a good Quantity of Hop-tops which are now in their greateſt Perfection, and tie them up in ſmall Bunches, twenty or thirty Tops in a Bunch, lay them in Spring Water for an Hour, ſhake them well, and lay them by; ſet on a ſmall Pot, pour into it three Quarts of thin Peaſe-ſoup deſcribed in our preceding Numbers, put in the Hop-tops, boil them well, then add four Spoonfuls of Juice of Onions, and ſome Pepper and Salt; boil the whole up again, and when it is enough ſet it off, ſoak ſome Cruſts in the Broth, and lay them in the Bottom of the Soup-Diſh; pour in the Soup, and garniſh the Diſh with the Hop-tops cut an Inch long.

This is the plain Hop-top Soup, and it is very good. The French often pour in ſome Cray-fiſh Cullis, and this gives it a great Richneſs, and quites alters its Nature. This is to be poured in hot when the Soup is in the Diſh.

4. *Onion Soup with Vinegar.*

Chuſe a dozen large and ſound Onions, peel them, cut them in Slices, and put them into a Stewpan with a little Butter; ſtew theſe together till they are brown, then duſt in ſome Flour, ſhake them about a little, and pour in a ſmall Quantity of Peaſe-ſoup; ſeaſon this well with Salt and Pepper, and let it boil half an Hour; pour in more Soup till there be enough for the Diſh, and then add ſome Vinegar to the Palate; there ſhould be enough to be taſted plainly, but not to make it very four.

Soak ſome Cruſts in Peaſe-ſoup, lay them in the Bottom of the Diſh, and then pour in the whole Quantity of the Soup.

5. *Savoy Soup.*

Chuſe five large Savoys, and cut each into four Quarters, boil them a little in Water, and ſtrain the Water off; when they are ſo cool that they can be handled, ſqueeze them dry of the Water.

U u 2

Put them into a Saucepan, and pour in as much Beef Gravy as will cover them ; fet the Saucepan on a moderate Fire, put on the Lid, and let them ſtew two Hours.

Set on a Saucepan with a quarter of a Pound of Butter, duſt in ſome Flour, and ſtir it about till it is brown ; then peel and mince a couple of Onions, put them into the Butter, and ſtir it well about again ; when theſe are pretty well done pour in a Quart of Veal Gravy, mix all well together, ſoak ſome Cruſts in the Gravy where the Savoys are ſtewed, and lay it in the Bottom of the Diſh, take out the Savoys, and lay them in the Diſh at ſmall Diſtances one from another, and pour in the Gravy and Onions, and ſerve it up

This is Savoy Soup plain, and a very rich and fine Diſh it is ; but there are Ways of making it richer.

6.   *Savoy Soup with a Duck.*

The Savoys are to be boiled in Water, and then ſtewed in Gravy firſt, as in the laſt Receipt, and the Gravy is to be prepared with Butter and Onions in the ſame Manner : When all this is in Readineſs a Duck is to be truſſed for boiling, and when ſo prepared it is to be fried brown all over, then it is to be put to ſtew in the Beef Gravy with the Savoys, and when all is done it is to be laid in the Middle of the Diſh with the Savoys round it.

In the ſame Manner the French ſometimes ſerve up a Pigeon in the Savoy Soup, ſtuffing the Breaſt with Force-Meat.

7.   *Muſcle Soup.*

Set on a Parcel of Muſcles in a Saucepan to ſtew in their own Liquor ; when they are half done take them up, reſerve a dozen or two that lie handſomeſt in the Shell for Garniſh. taking off the empty Shell, and leaving the Muſcle in the other.

Pick

Pick out all the reft, and put them into a Stewpan with a little of their own Liquor, add to them fome Parfley fhred fine, fome Chibols minced fmall, and half a dozen whole Cloves; put in with thefe a Piece of Butter, and let all ftew well together.

When the Mufcles are well done pour in fome Fifh Cullis defcribed in its Place, and about a third Part of the Quantity of Cray-fifh Cullis; let the whole be as much as will fuit the Size of the Difh; make all hot together, and in the mean Time foak fome Crufts in Fifh Broth; lay thefe in the Bottom of the Difh, pour in the Soup with the Mufcles in it, and garnifh with the Mufcles in their Shells faved for that Purpofe and kept hot.

C H A P. IX.

Of Gravies.

A R T. I. *Beef Gravy with Mufhrooms.*

CHUSE a dozen and half of very large Flaps, that is the biggeft full-opened Mufhrooms that can be got, cut out the Stalks, peel off the Skin, fcrape away the Gills, and then ftrew them over with Pepper and a little Salt; cut fome thick Beef Steaks from a good Part of the Beef where there is little Fat; the Leg of Mutton Piece is very proper for this Purpofe; let there be five or fix Pounds of thefe Steaks, and let them be an Inch thick.

Beat thefe well, and feafon them moderately with Pepper and Salt.

Set on a large Stewpan, lay in the Bottom of it half a dozen Slices of fat Bacon, fo as to cover the Bottom, upon thefe lay four or five of the Mufhrooms, then lay in fome of the Beef Steaks, upon thefe lay the reft of the Mufhrooms, and the reft of the Beef Steaks over them; then cut to Pieces four Onions, and fcat-

ter

ter them among the Beef, cut alfo four Carrots to
Pieces and throw them in; cover up the Stewpan,
and fet it over a gentle Fire; let all ftew together for
fome Time, and watch how the Gravy comes; when
there is a good deal fet it on a better Fire, and let it
boil away till the Meat is nearly dry, it will then
begin to ftick to the Pan; uncover it, ftir all about,
and put the Carrots and other Roots undermoft that
they may get brown; when they are browned, but
not burnt, pour in fome good Broth, or common
Gravy, made of a Leg of Beef, as before directed;
then boil all up together with a whole Leek, fome
Parfley, and half a dozen Cloves; boil it well, and
then ftrain it off through a Sieve for Ufe.

It is an exceeding rich Gravy for Soups and Made
Difhes, far exceeding the moft coftly Gravies of the
French, into which they put Partridges and Wood-
cocks; the Mufhroom with the Beef is richer.

CHAP. X.

Of Made Difhes.

WE fhall here deliver Rules for making the
moft elegant as well as the moft excellent
Made Difhes, and fhall endeavour to comprife the
moft pompous within a moderate Expence.   There
will be a Difference between thofe for fmaller and
thofe for larger Families, but we fhall moderate the
Charge greatly even in the moft pompous, and at the
fame Time defcribe them as they have been ferved
up to the Satisfaction of the greateft Judges in fine
eating: Knowledge will go farther than Expence in
all thefe Matters.

A R T. I. *An Olio the French Way.*

Cut into thick Steaks five Pounds of the Leg of
Mutton Piece of Beef, put this into a deep Stewpan,
add to it five Pounds of fome ordinary Part of Veal,
and

and a Leg of Mutton of fix or feven Pounds; this laft muft be fkinned, and the Fat taken away; cover up the Stewpan, and fet it over a Stove with a moderate Fire, let it ftand till the Gravy is come, then brifk up the Fire a little, and keep it on till the Meat begins to ftick to the Pan, but do not let it ftand longer, for it is not to be browned over much; when it is beginning to ftick pour in a little Beef Gravy, and ftir it about.

When the Gravy is well mixed and coloured put all into a Pot, fet it on the Fire covered up, and put in more Gravy to fill the Pot near full; then cut to Pieces a dozen Carrots, nine Parfnips, eight good Onions, and half a dozen Turnips; put all thefe into the Pot, and add to them a Bunch of Leeks, a Bundle of Celeri, and a Handful of the fweet Mignonette, an Herb common in France, and now kept in fome of our Gardens; let all thefe boil well together, then put in a Fowl, a Turkey, and a Brace of Pigeons; add two Pounds of Ham cut in thick Slices, and keep all this boiling well, often fkimming it when the leaft Foulnefs rifes.

While thefe are boiling together take four French Rolls well baked and rafped, pare the Cruft carefully off, and put it into a Stewpan with a little of the Olio Liquor; when they are foft put them into an Olio Pot, or they may be fent up in a Tureen, or in a very deep Soup-Difh, pour on the Broth, and let there be among it a little of the Celeri, and fome fmall Pieces of the Roots of all the Kinds, and add fome choice Pieces of the other Ingredients, and the Pigeons entire.

This is the plain French Olio, and it is a very fine Difh.

They often make it richer, by boiling a Brace of Partridges in the Gravy, and putting a Brace more roafted for that Purpofe in the Difh; but it is excellent without thefe.

2. *A Spanish Olio.*

The Olioes were an Invention of the Spaniards, and their Receipts, though particular in some Things, are much richer and better than the French, or those of any other Nation; this which follows is the principal and finest of all.

Cut out some Gristle from a Brisket of Beef, and some Gristle from a Breast of Veal and from a Breast of Mutton, cut to Pieces some Sheeps Rumps, and cut these Gristles also into Pieces of the Bigness of a Finger.

Cut five Pounds of Beef into Steaks, put these and the Gristles into a Pot, and pour upon them a good Quantity of strong Beef Broth, put in with them a Bunch of Leeks, and a large Bunch of Celeri picked very clean.

Let this stew till the Rumps and Gristles are tender, and then put in two Pigeons, a Brace of Partridges, two Pair of Hogs Feet and Ears, the Knuckle End of a Ham, and half a fine white Cabbage; put in some Pepper and Salt, a Bunch of sweet Basil, a couple of Onions, and some Cloves; cover all this with some fresh Beef Steaks cut thick, and over that lay two Pounds of fresh Veal cut also into Steaks, pour in a little fresh Broth upon these, and leave them to stew upon a gentle Fire; let the whole stand stewing till all the Liquor is evaporated, and the Ingredients begin to stick to the Bottom, then put in some more Broth.

While this is doing let some large Pease that have been soaked four and twenty Hours in Water be set on to boil in a Saucepan, with some Beef Gravy.

The Spaniards use a particular Sort of Pease they call Garavances; they are large, and not unlike our grey Pease; but, if these are not to be had, any large Pea will do.

Let these be boiled till very tender in the Gravy, and let them be ready when the Olio is. The last

Broth

Broth that is put in muſt boil a quarter of an Hour with the Ingredients, and then all is done. Seaſon it to the Palate with Pepper and Salt, and ſet the Diſh ready: This ſhould be a very large and deep Soup-Diſh, or elſe a Pot made for that Purpoſe.

Firſt take out the ſeveral Ingredients one by one, and lay them handſomely in the Diſh, ſo that they may ſet off one another; the Griſtles and the Roots muſt be diſpoſed in different Parts among the others: When every Thing is well diſpoſed pour over them the Peaſe and their Gravy, and then pour in a proper Quantity of the Liquor, but not too much. Remember it is not a Soup, but an Olio, the Things are to be eaten in Preference of the Liquor.

For ſuch as like more of the Liquor ſend up ſeveral Baſons of it covered, with a Piece of Bread nicely toaſted on the Cover. This is the true Spaniſh Olio.

3. *A Shoulder of Mutton in Epigram.*

Lay down a good large Shoulder of Mutton to roaſt.

While it is roaſting mix together ſome Crumbs of Bread and Leaves of Thyme and Sweet Marjoram ſtripped from the Stalks, ſome Lemon Peel ſhred very ſmall, ſome ſhred Parſley, and Pepper and Salt, with a little grated Nutmeg.

Let theſe lie ready on a Plate, and have a clear Fire and a Gridiron heated alſo in Readineſs.

When the Mutton is nearly enough raiſe the Skin all over, of the Thickneſs of a Crown Piece, looſen it perfectly every where without breaking it, and then cut off the Shank Bone ſo as to take the whole Skin with it.

Seaſon this thick Skin very thoroughly with the Bread Crumbs and Spices mixed for that Purpoſe, and lay it on the Gridiron at a good Diſtance from the Fire; ſtrew more of the Crumbs and Spices upon it as it is on, and do the ſame when it is turned;

Nº. XII.   X x   obſerve

obferve that it is to be thoroughly done, and at the laft is to be finely browned.

While this is doing cut all the Meat off the Shoulder into thin Pieces as for a fine Hafh, and fave all the Gravy ; put this cut Meat into a Saucepan, and put in all its own Gravy, and a Cup full of ftrong Gravy befide ; put in with it half an Onion, fome Pepper and Salt, fome grated Nutmeg, and a Bundle of fweet Herbs ; let all this ftew together fome Time, but don't let it boil ; when this is done tolerably take out the fweet Herbs, and put in fome pickled Cucumbers cut fmall, and fome Mufhrooms and Truffles ; laft of all add half a Glafs of red Wine, and duft in a very little Flour ; let it ftew fome Minutes, and the while let the broiled Part be carefully done ; when all is ready let the Hafh be laid in a Difh, and the broiled Part over it.

This is a very pretty Difh, with a very particular Name ; but it is very well liked, if not very well underftood.

4. *A Leg of Mutton a la Haut-Gout.*

Chufe a fine large Leg of Mutton of ten Pounds, or more, hang it up in a cool airy Place as long as it will keep, and after the five or fix firft Days examine it from Time to Time that it be not fpoiled ; it will in tolerable Weather keep ten Days, fometimes a Fortnight.

When it is in the Condition of a Haunch of Venifon for roafting take it down, and ftick it all over with Cloves of Garlick, then rub it well with Pepper and Salt, and roaft it.

When it is near enough fet on a Saucepan with fome Gravy, when it is hot break in a Stick of Cinnamon, add to this a Glafs of red Wine, and fend it up with the Mutton.

5. *A Fricaffee of Neats Tongues.*

Boil a couple of Neats Tongues till they are perfectly tender, then peel them, cut them into thin Slices, and fry them in frefh Butter; when they are done enough put them into another Stewpan with fome rich Veal Gravy, put in with them a Bundle of fweet Herbs and an Onion, two Blades of Mace, and fome Salt and Pepper; let thefe ftew together a quarter of an Hour, then take out the Tongues, ftrain the Gravy, and put both into the Stewpan again.

Break a couple of Eggs, and beat up the Yolks with a Glafs of white Wine; grate in a little Nutmeg, roll a Piece of Butter in Flour, and put this with the Eggs into the Stewpan; fhake all about for five Minutes, and then fend it up.

6. *A Leg of Mutton with Oifters.*

Cut very fine half a Pound of Mutton Suet, mix with it fome Salt, fome Pepper, a little grated Nutmeg, and the Yolks of four Eggs boiled hard for that Purpofe.

When this is ready ftick a Leg of Mutton with Cloves, ftuff it with this Mixture, and lay it down to roaft.

When the Mutton is half done cut off fome fmall Pieces from the under Side of the flefhy End, and put thefe into a fmall Saucepan; put with them a Pint of Oifters, let all the Liquor of the Oifters be put in with them, and let there be added two Blades of Mace, a little Bay Salt, and half a Pint of boiling Water.

Stew thefe well till a good Part of the Liquor is wafted, and then take them off; when the Meat is enough take it up, then put a Piece of Butter rolled in Flour into the Saucepan, fhake all well together, and pour it over the Mutton; fend it up hot, and it is a very excellent Way of eating Mutton.

7. *A*

7.   *A Raggoo of Lamb.*

Cut off the Knuckle of a fore Quarter of Lamb, then lard the reſt very well with Bacon, grate a little Nutmeg over it, ſqueeze on this the Juice of half a Seville Orange, and ſet it on in a Stewpan with a little Butter, and fry it to a fine brown.

When this is done take it out of that Stewpan and put it into one that is deeper, add to it three Pints of Veal Gravy, four Blades of Mace, four Cloves, a Spoonful of whole Pepper, ſome Shreds of Lemon Peel, and a ſmall Bundle of ſweet Herbs; cover this up, ſet it on a pretty briſk Fire, and let it boil and ſtew moderately half an Hour.

Then pour off the Gravy, and keep the Lamb in the Pot hot.

As the Gravy cools ſkim off the Fat from its Top.

Take half a Pint of large Oiſters without their Liquor, flour them, and then fry them in Butter; when they are pretty well done pour off the Butter, and then pour in the Gravy to the Oiſters; put in at the ſame Time an Anchovy boned and cut to Pieces, and a Glaſs of red Port Wine; let this boil till a good deal of the Liquor is waſted, then throw in ſome freſh Muſhrooms picked and cleaned, put in alſo ſome pickled ones, and a Spoonful of the Liquor, and add the Juice of half a Lemon; when all this is ready take out the Lamb which has been all the while kept hot, lay it handſomely in a Diſh, and pour the Sauce over it; then garniſh it with Lemon.

8.   *Pillaw of Veal.*

Lay down a Neck of Veal, and half roaſt it; when it is thus far done take it off the Spit, cut it into five or ſix Pieces, and ſeaſon it with Pepper and Salt, and a little Nutmeg.

Set on a Stewpan with the Bottom buttered, put in a Quart of rich Broth and a Pound of Rice, add two

Blades

Blades of Mace, a Nutmeg broke in a Mortar into four or five Pieces, fome Pepper, and fome Salt; fet this on a flow Fire, and let it ftew till the whole is thick and the Rice tender; when this is near done break eight Eggs, beat up the Yolks, mix them with fome of the Stew, and then add them to the whole.

Butter the Bottom and Sides of a fmall deep Soup-Difh, lay in a good Quantity of the prepared Rice at the Bottom, upon this lay the Pieces of Veal one upon another in a little Heap, then pour in the reft of the Rice, beat up the Yolks of three more Eggs, and cover the whole with them.

In this Condition fend it to be baked, and let it remain in a moderate Oven half an Hour; when it comes home have half a Pint of rich Veal Gravy ready hot, open the Pillaw at the Top, and pour in the Gravy, then fend it up, garnifhed with Lemon cut to Pieces and quartered.

9. *Olives of Veal the French Way.*

Cut into fmall Pieces, of about three Fingers Breadth and a Finger's Thicknefs, three Pounds of fine Veal, chop to Pieces a quarter of a Pound of Beef Marrow, wafh a couple of Anchovies, take out the Bones, and cut them to Pieces, mix this with the Marrow, grate over it fome Nutmeg, break to Pieces the Yolks of two Eggs boiled hard for that Purpofe, chop to Pieces fome frefh Mufhrooms, and a dozen and half of large Oifters without the Beards, ftrip fome Thyme and Sweet Marjoram Leaves from the Stalks, add fome Salt, Pepper, and beaten Mace, and mix all well together.

Have a Veal Caul clean and ready, and cut fome thin Slices of very fat Bacon; when all this is ready begin to put the whole together.

Spread the Caul open, and lay in fome Slices of Bacon nearly to cover it, then put upon this a thin Covering of the Ingredients, upon this lay fome of the Veal, and upon that fome more of the Ingredients, then fome Bacon again, and fo on till all is in; then

roll

roll up the Caul with the whole in it, and roaft it; let the Fire be brifk, and an Hour will do it.

When it is near enough make the Sauce thus:

Set on fome very good Gravy, add to it a little Effence of Ham, and thicken it with fome Cullis.

When the Meat is taken up cut it into thick Slices all together, lay them handfomely in a Difh, and pour the Gravy over it hot; garnifh this with Lemon fliced and quartered.

10. *Sweetbreads a la Dauphine.*

Chufe three very large and fine Sweetbreads; this Number makes a very handfome Difh.

Roaft a large Fowl, and cut off all the Flefh from the Breaft, cut half a Pound of Bacon, Fat and Lean together, in very thin Slices, and mince thefe extremely fmall; when thefe are mixed together put them into a Marble Mortar, put in with them an Anchovy, wafhed, boned, and cut to Pieces; add fome Lemon Peel fhred very fine, fome fhred Parfley, and a little grated Nutmeg.

Beat all thefe well together in the Mortar, and when they are thoroughly mixed put in as much Yolk of Eggs as will make them a good firm Pafte.

This is the proper Force-meat for the ftuffing of a Sweetbread.

When it is thus got ready open the three Sweetbreads, ftuff them well with it, and then faften them together with fine fmall wooden Skewers.

Set on a Stewpan, lay in the Bottom of it fome thin Slices of fat Bacon, ftrew over them a Seafoning of Salt and Pepper, with fome bruifed Cloves and Mace, and laft of all fcatter upon them fome Slices of Onion cut into very fmall and thin Slices; lay upon this Seafoning, or rather upon the Bacon thus feafoned, fome very thin Slices of Veal, and upon thefe lay the Sweetbreads; cover the Stewpan clofe, and fet it over a flow Fire ten Minutes.

When

When the Stewpan is set on let there be a Saucepan set on also with a Quart of Broth; this will boil by that Time the Sweetbreads are ready for it, and it must then be poured gently into the Pan; let this be covered up, and set over a very gentle Fire to stew for two Hours.

Then uncover the Pan, and take out the Sweetbreads.

Strain off the Gravy, which will now be very fine, skim off the Fat, and boil it till there is not more than half a Pint left.

When it is thus rich put in the Sweetbreads, let them stew in it five Minutes that all may be hot together, then take them out, lay them regularly in a Dish, and pour the Gravy over them; garnish the Dish with Quarters of Lemon cut thin.

C H A P. XI.

Of Puddings.

W E shall here, as in the former Chapters, add some Receipts for the better Sort of Puddings from long Experience.

A R T. I. *Lemon Pudding.*

Chuse a couple of large fresh and fine Lemons, grate down all the Peel; grate to Powder also two Naples Biscuits, mix these together, then add to them three quarters of a Pound of treble-refined Sugar powdered.

Break twelve Eggs and throw away half the Whites, beat up the twelve Yolks and six Whites, and by Degrees mix with them a Pint of rich Cream and three quarters of a Pound of melted Butter.

When these are well mixed together bring in the Powder by Degrees, and when all is in let it be well mixed.

Cover

Cover a Diſh with fine Puff-paſte Cruſt, and put in the whole; ſend it to the Oven, and give Directions that it be put in when the Heat is moderate. An Hour will do it.

2.   *A Sagoe Pudding.*

Pick thoroughly clean half a Pound of Sagoe, pour a Quart of ſcalding Water upon it, ſtir it well, and then pour off the Water. Waſh it in this Manner three Times, and then put it into a Saucepan; break in two Sticks of Cinnamon, and pour to it a Quart of Milk; boil theſe together till it is all thick, but this muſt be done with great Care, for if it be not ſtirred continually it will burn. When it is thick enough ſtir in half a Pound of Butter.

Then break nine Eggs, take all the Yolks and five of the Whites, beat them up with a Glaſs of Mountain and a little grated Nutmeg, pour the Sagoe into a Pan, and mix the Eggs with it.

Pick a quarter of a Pound of Currants, and lay them to plump in hot Water. Sweeten the Sagoe thus mixed with the other Ingredients, then ſtir in a Glaſs of Roſe-water and a Glaſs of Sack, and laſt of all the Currants.

Cover a Diſh with Puff-paſte, pour in the whole, and ſend it to be baked. It muſt have a moderate Oven and good Time.

3.   *Millet Pudding.*

Powder half a Pound of Loaf-ſugar and ſift it, waſh half a Pound of Millet, and when it is clean and wiped dry between two Cloths, mix it with the Sugar; mix theſe with two Quarts of Milk, grate in a whole Nutmeg, and add half a Pound of freſh Butter broke to Pieces; the whole to be well mixed, and it will then be ready for the Diſh. Let a Diſh be well buttered, and pour it in, ſend it to the Oven, and let it be baked an Hour and a quarter in a moderate Degree of Heat.

4.   *Pearl-*

4. *Pearl-Barley Pudding.*

Wash a Pound of Pearl-Barley in several scalding Waters, then put it into a Pan with three Quarts of Milk, and add half a Pound of Lump-sugar beat to Powder, and a whole grated Nutmeg; send this to the Oven when Bread is to be baked, and let it stand the Time of the Loaves.

Then take it out of the Pan, beat up six Eggs and mix well with it, butter a Dish, and pour in the Pudding; send it again to the Oven for half an Hour, and it will come back in excellent Order, and is a delicate cheap Pudding.

5. *A Batter Pudding.*

Break six Eggs, beat up all the Yolks with half the Whites, add to these a Tea Spoonful of Salt and the same Quantity of powdered Ginger, mix them well together, and then mix in six large Spoonfuls of Flour, and by Degrees a Quart of Milk.

Put this up in a Bag and boil it a quarter of an Hour, and when it is taken up pour plain melted Butter over it, but let it be carefully and well melted.

6. *A Custard Pudding.*

Mix together three Spoonfuls of Cream and one Spoonful of Flour, set on a Pint of Cream to boil, when it boils take it off, pour it into a Bason, and mix the Cream and Flour well with it.

While this is cooling break five Eggs, beat up all the Yolks and two of the Whites, and mix with them a Glass of Sack, a little Salt, some grated Nutmeg, and as much powdered Sugar as will well sweeten the Puddding.

Butter the Inside of a wooden Bowl.

When the Cream is thoroughly cold mix in these Igredients with it, and then pour all into the Bowl.

Tie a Cloth over it, and boil it half an Hour.

C H A P. XII.

Of Pies.

THE Cook will find, under all thefe Articles, that there is a great Variety of Things to be done ; and having acquainted herfelf with doing the plaineft firft, fhe will find no Difficulty in the richeft of the others.

A R T. I. *Lobfter Pie.*

Boil a couple of large and fine Lobfters, and while they are boiling cover a Difh of a proper Bignefs with a good Cruft.

When the Lobfters are enough break them up, feparate the Tail, fplit it, take out the Gut, and then cut each into four Pieces. Lay thefe regularly in the Difh.

Break the Claws and pick out the Flefh, open the Body, and pick every thing clean out of that ; chop, break, and mix all this very well together ; grate in a little Nutmeg, feafon it with Pepper and Salt, and a little Vinegar ; rub the Crumb of a Halfpenny Roll to Powder, and mix with this ; then melt half a Pound of Butter, and work it in.

When all is thus done lay the whole upon the Tails in the Difh and put on a Cover, fend it to be baked in a flack Oven, and about half an Hour will be fufficient.

2. *Salmon Pie.*

Lobfter is an Ingredient of great Confequence in a Salmon Pie, and the whole is in fome Meafure of the Nature of the laft mentioned, but it is much richer ; make it thus.

Firft prepare a very good Cruft, according to the Directions given under that Head in a former Number.

Then

Then chuse a prime Piece of frefh Salmon, clean it perfectly, and wafh it laft of all with a Spunge wetted in white Wine; put fome Cruft round the Difh, but none at the Bottom; only butter the Bottom of the Difh, and then lay in the Salmon. After feafoning it very well with Pepper and Salt grate a little Nutmeg over it, and add two Blades of Mace bruifed.

Boil a Lobfter, take out all the Flefh, mix that and the Infide of the Body together, melt half a Pound of frefh Butter, and mix all the Lobfter perfectly well with it; then put this into the Difh over the Salmon, and then put on the Lid; fend it to be baked, and let it ftand an Hour in a moderate Oven.

3. *Salt Fifh Pie.*

Chufe a fine Side of falt Fifh, lay it in Water all Night, and then boil it till it is fomewhat tender; take it out of the Water, and lay it on a Cloth.

As foon as it is cool ftrip off the Skin, and get the Flefh from the Bones. Mince this very fine. While this is doing fet on a Quart of Milk with the Crumb of two French Rolls, break the Bread thoroughly in the Milk with a Spoon, and then mix in the falt Fifh minced as before directed; ftir all very well together.

Melt a Pound of Butter and mix with this, chop very fine as much Parfley as will make two Spoonfuls, and mix this in; grate in half a Nutmeg, and add a little Pepper and three Tea Spoonfuls of Muftard. Mix all thefe well together, and then put them into a Difh; cover them with a good Cruft, and bake it well.

4. *A Soal Pie.*

Clean and fkin three good large Eels, boil them in as little Water as will ferve for that Purpofe, and when they are enough take them up, pick the Flefh clean from the Bones, and throw the Bones into the Water again; boil them well, pepper and falt the Liquor, and reduce it to a quarter of a Pint; it will be then very rich, and ftrong of the Fifh.

Mince

Mince the Flesh of the Eel while this is boiling away, make it very fine, and mix with it some Lemon-peel cut very fine, some Pepper and Salt, a quarter of a Nutmeg grated, and some Crumbs of Bread. Wash an Anchovy, take out the Bone, chop the Flesh small and mix with it, then melt a quarter of a Pound of Butter and mix with the whole. Last of all put in a Spoonful of chopped Parsley.

When this Force-meat is made prepare your Crust, cover a Dish well with it, and then put in the Force-meat.

Then chuse three Pair of moderately large Soals, pick the Flesh from the Bones, and lay it upon the Force-meat.

Strain off the rich Gravy of the Eel, and pour that over the whole, then put on the Lid, and send it to the Oven. It will be an excellent and rich Dish.

5. *A Rabbit Pie.*

Chuse a couple of fine Rabbits, take out the Livers, and save them, clean the Rabbits perfectly, cut off the Heads, and the first Joints of the Legs, then lard them well with fat and fine Bacon; season them with Pepper and Salt, a couple of Blades of Mace bruised, and some Leaves of Thyme and sweet Marjoram picked from the Stalks.

Make a good Crust, lay in the Rabbits cut in half, but first garnish the Bottom with scrap'd Bacon; when the Rabbits are in sprinkle upon them a few Chives cut small, and some chopped Parsley; put a Bunch of sweet Herbs with them, and lay over them some thin Slices of Veal, and some large thin Slices of Bacon.

Put on the Top, and send the Pie to the Oven.

While it is baking make Cullis purposely for it, in this Manner:

Cut a Pound of Fillet of Veal into thin Slices, and put with it a Piece of Gammon of Bacon; lay these

in

in the Bottom of a Stewpan, with fome fliced Onions and Carrots, and lay the Livers of the Rabbits over them.

Cover the Stewpan, and fet it over a Stove with a moderate Heat; when the Livers are foft take them out, and pound them in a Marble Mortar.

Let the other Ingredients remain till they begin to ftick to the Pan; then throw in a little melted Bacon, duft in a very little Flour, and pour in a fmall Quantity of boiling Water; ftir it about.

Then pour in fome good Broth, and at the fame Time put in a whole Leek, a Bundle of fweet Herbs, fome Blades of Mace, and three or four beaten Cloves; add fome Mufhrooms and fome Truffles; and laft of all put in fome Crufts of Bread; let all fcimmer together, and fo continue it half an Hour.

Then take out the Slices of Veal, put in the pounded Livers, and ftir all well about together; when it is well mixed ftrain it through a Sieve, put it into a Saucepan, and keep it hot, but do not let it boil.

When the Pie comes home open it, take out the Veal, and pour in the Cullis quite hot, put on the Lid again, and ferve it up for a firft Courfe. It is a very rich and elegant Difh.

C H A P. XIII.

Side and fmall Difhes.

WE fhall add to the Number we have before defcribed of thefe fome very elegant ones, and fuch as are not fo expenfive as to place them beyond the Ufe of a moderate genteel Family.

A R T.   I.   *Lobfter Patties.*

Boil a couple of Lobfters, get out all the Flefh, and chop and mix it perfectly well together.

Throw

Throw the Shells, the fmall Claws, and the Spawn, if there be any, into a Marble Mortar, and pound it well.

Then put to it the Cruft of a French Roll, pound it again, and pour in a quarter of a Pint of rich Broth; then put it into a Saucepan, pour on a little more Broth, and feaſon it with Pepper and Salt; fet it on to boil, let it continue boiling till it is thick, then ftrain it through a Sieve, and dividing it into two equal Parts, put one half to the Lobfters, and fave the other in a Bafon.

Squeeze a little Lemon into the Lobfters thus mixed up, add fome Pepper and Salt, half an Anchovy, and a Piece of Butter.

Warm all this over the Fire that the Butter may be melted, and all well mixed; then fet it by to cool.

Make a fine Cruft, and cover the Bottom of fome fmall Patty-pans, then put in the Lobfter, and cover it with a Lid; fend it to the Oven in Time, that it may be well done, and come home in Time.

When it is come back heat the half of the Gravy that was faved in the Bafon, put a Piece of Butter to it, and then take off the Lid of the Pie; pour in this Gravy, then cut the Lid in two, and lay it on again, but let the two Pieces lie at a little Diftance that the Lobfter may be feen between them.

This is a fine fecond Courfe Difh.

2. *Muſhroom Patties.*

Get a Quantity of good middle-fized Muſhrooms, pick them clean, fcrape out the Gills, peel them, and then put them into a Saucepan, with fome Pepper and Salt, a Piece of Bacon ftuck with four Cloves, fome chopped Parfley, a whole Onion, and a quarter of a Pound of Butter.

Put them over a moderate Fire, cover the Saucepan clofe, and let them ftew a little; then open the Saucepan, duft in a little Flour, and cover it up
again;

again; fhake them about from Time to Time, and take Care that they do not burn.

In fome Time the Liquor will be as thick as Cream; then pour all out into a Bafon, take away the Onion and the Bacon, and leave the reft to cool.

Make fome good Pafte, roll it out to the Thick-nefs of a Halfpenny, cover a Tart-pan with it, and then put in the cold Mufhrooms; cover it with a Sheet of Pafte a little thicker than that at the Bottom, and fend it to the Oven in Time.

When it comes home take off the Cover, and fqueeze in half a Lemon; put the Cover on again, and ferve it up.

There is a very pretty Way of baking Mufhrooms in this Manner, but without a Top Cruft. For this Purpofe all muft be done juft as before, but, inftead of the Cover, fpread over the Mufhrooms a Coat of brown Rafpings of a French Roll; when this is baked fqueeze half a Lemon over it, and then fend it up hot.

3. *Patty of Calves Brains.*

Take the Brains clean from a couple of Calves Heads, clean them very carefully, and then fcald them; cut fome fine young Afparagus Tops, blanch them in a Saucepan with fome Parfley and Butter, and boil fix Eggs hard, take out the Yolks, mix thefe with an equal Quantity of Force-meat, and put them to the Brains, then mix the Afparagus with the reft.

Cover a Patty-pan with a Sheet of thin Cruft, put in this Mixture, and cover it up, fend it to the Oven, and when it comes home raife up the Cover and fqueeze in the Juice of half a Lemon; then pour in fome drawn Butter and Gravy, and ferve it up.

4. *Collops*

4. *Collops and Eggs.*

Cut fome very thin Slices of hung Mutton, and broil them carefully, when they are done lay them evenly on a Dish, and fet them before the Fire to keep hot.

Have a Stewpan of boiling Water on a Stove, or on another Part of the Fire, break as many Eggs as there are Collops or broiled Slices of Meat, break thefe one by one into a clean China Cup, and put them into the Water in the Stewpan.

Watch when the Whites begin to harden, and when they are of a good Colour, and look clear, take them out.

Get an Egg-Slice under them one by one for this Purpofe, and as they are taken out and drained upon the Slice, lay them one by one upon the Collops, one Egg on each.

This is the proper Way of eating Eggs and Bacon alfo, the Eggs being poached, and the Bacon broiled in this Manner.

5. *Salmagundy.*

Pick and wash three good Dutch Lettuces, cut them as fine as Threads, and lay them at the Bottom of a Dish.

Cut the Flesh from the Breasts of a couple of roasted Chickens; it must be cut into Slices as long and broad as one's Finger, and not thicker than a Shilling; fpread thefe carefully over the Lettuces in regular Circles, leaving Spaces between them.

Wash and bone half a dozen fine Anchovies, cut each into eight Pieces, and lay thefe regularly between the Slices of Chicken.

Then cut the Legs of the Chickens into fmall fquare Pieces like Dice, and cut a good Lemon into fquare Pieces in the fame Manner.

Boil four Eggs hard, take out the Yolks, mince them, and mix with them fome chopped Parfley and four Anchovies minced very fmall.

Boil

Boil fome Onions, as big as Wallnuts, till they are very white and tender.

Then pile up the minced Anchovy and Egg in the Middle of the Diſh like a little Sugar-Loaf, lay the Onions round it, and lay others thick round the Edge of the Diſh.

When all is thus done, mix fome Oil and Vinegar very well, beating it up with Salt and Pepper, and pour it carefully over the whole Diſh, then ferve it up.

It is not only very foon ready for eating, but makes a pretty Appearance: There is as much Nicety of Hand ſhewn in dreſſing up a Salmagundy as in any Thing.

6.   *Petit Patties with Carrot.*

Mince the Kidney of a Loin of Veal, and as much of the Fat about it as is equal to its own Weight; mince fome boiled Carrot very fine, and mix with this.

Mince the Yolks of two Eggs boiled hard, and grate in a quarter of a Nutmeg, ſtrew over fome Pepper and Salt, with a very little beaten Mace, and then fome Sugar.

When all theſe are perfectly well mixed together cut a very large and fine Seville Orange, and ſqueeze the Juice carefully all over them; if any of the Seeds fall in take them out; roll this up in Puff Paſte Cruſt, and fry it in Lard. This Quantity will very well make four Patties.

SECT. III.

Of CONFECTIONARY.

CHAP. I.

Of Creams.

WE have many elegant Things to add under this Head, and ſhall give fome in every Return of this Chapter.

A R T. I. *Steeple Cream.*

PUT into a large Stone Bottle five Ounces of the fineſt large Hartſhorn Shavings, and two Ounces and a half of clean and thin Shavings of Ivory, two Ounces of Gum Arabick, and an Ounce of beaten Iſinglaſs; fill up the Bottle with Water nearly to the Topp, ſtop it, and tie it over with Leather.

Set on a large Pot of Water, with a Wiſp of clean Straw at the Bottom; put the Stone Bottle into the Pot of Water, and let it boil.

Keep the Pot upon the Fire ſix Hours, ſupplying more boiling Water as it waſtes, and keep it boiling all the Time; then ſet it off to cool, take out the Stone Bottle, and when it is perfeᷱly cold open it.

Blanch a Pound of ſweet Almonds, and beat them to a Paſte in a Marble Mortar; mix with this Paſte a Pint of rich Cream.

Strain off the Liquor in the Bottle, and it will be a thick Jelly.

Mix the Cream and Almonds with a Pound of the Jelly, and ſet them together over the Fire till they are ſcalding hot; when this is done ſweeten it to the Taſte with very fine Sugar, add a few Drops of Eſſence of Ambergreaſe, and pour it into ſome high Jelly Pots, broad at the Top and narrow at the Bottom. When it is cold it will be firm, and ſo fit to ſet upright in a Diſh, where it will reſemble a Sugar-Loaf or a Steeple. Lay ſome whipp'd Cream cool about the Steeples, and they make a very pretty Appearance.

2. *Almond Cream.*

Set on a Quart of rich Cream in a clean Saucepan, put into it a Blade of Mace, and a Piece of Lemon Peel, grate in a third Part of a Nutmeg, and ſweeten it to your Taſte.

Blanch a Quarter of a Pound of ſweet Almonds, and beat them to a Paſte; add to them in beating

two

two Spoonfuls of Rofe Water, and one Spoonful of Orange-Flower Water.

Break nine Eggs, feparate the Yolks for other Ufes, beat up all the Whites, and mix them with the Almonds; beat all well together, and rub the whole through a coarfe Hair Sieve.

Mix all together with the Cream, and fet it over the Fire, ftir it only one Way, and let it boil; then pour it off into Cups, Difhes, or Glaffes, and ferve it up: It looks very pretty, and taftes very agreeably.

3. *Sweet Cream.*

Put into a Saucepan a Pint of Cream, fweeten it with double-refined Sugar powdered, grate in a little Nutmeg, and add two Spoonfuls of Orange-Flower Water.

Break four Eggs, beat up all the four Yolks and two of the Whites, and add to them a Glafs of Sack; mix this with the Cream, and then fet it over the Fire till it is thick, ftirring it only one Way.

When it is enough pour it into Cups.

5. *Ratafia Cream.*

Break five Eggs, beat up the Yolks with fome cold Cream, and with a large Spoonful of the fineft Sugar powdered.

Set on a Quart of thick Cream in a Saucepan, and put on fix Laurel Leaves; when it has once boiled up throw away the Leaves, and put in the Eggs beat up as already directed; ftir all together, and keep it hot fome Time, but without letting it boil, and obferve to ftir it only one Way, and when it is thick enough pour it into Cups or China Bowls for the Table.

5. *Moonfhine.*

As the Shape and Appearance is of great Confequence in this Difh, Care muft be firft taken about that: Some Tin Moulds muft be made for this Purpofe, or Copper ones tinned all over: They will coft no great Matter, and will laft for ever.

One

One of thefe, which is the Principal, muft be of the Shape of a new Moon, and as deep as a half Pint Bafon, but without any Bottom; another muft be made in the Shape of a large Star with its Rays, and there muft be two or three leffer Stars.

This will be fufficient, and it is very well worth while to have them in every genteel Family.

Chufe a couple of fine Calf's Feet, clean them, fet them on in a Gallon of Water, and boil them gently till there is but about a Quart left.

Then ftrain this off, fkim away the Fat, and it will be a ftrong Jelly.

Separate this into two Halves, fweeten one half to your Palate, and beat up the Whites of four Eggs, put them in, and fet it over the Fire till it boils.

Strain it off, and repeat this again and again through a Jelly-bag, till it is perfectly clear.

While this is doing blanch an Ounce of Almonds, beat them to a Pafte in a Marble Mortar, with a Spoonful of Rofe Water, and the fame Quantity of Orange-Flower Water; fqueeze this through a coarfe Cloth, and mix it with the Jelly.

Set it over the Fire again, ftir in three large Spoon-fuls of rich and thick Cream, and let it ftand on the Fire till it boils.

Prepare the Difh it is to be ferved up in, lay the half Moon in the Middle, the great Star in the Hollow between its Points or Horns, and the fmall Stars round it; put fome Pieces of Lead upon the Moon and Stars that they keep flat upon the Bottom of the Difh, and pour in the Jelly, which is by this Mixture made into a Kind of what the French call Blanc Manger.

When this is quite cold take out the Things, and the Blanc Manger will retain the Shape, and ftand very firm in it.

Then fet on the half of the Jelly that was faved to heat, put into it half a Pint of Mountain Wine, and the Juice of three Lemons, and fweeten it with the fineft Sugar powdered.

Break

Break eight Eggs, and beat up the Whites with a little of the Jelly, pour them in to the reſt and let it all boil; when all is well mixed ſtir it once together, and pour it into a Jelly-bag; ſtrain it over and over till it is perfeEtly fine, and then pour it into the Diſh.

There will be Spaces between the Moon and Stars where the Moulds ſtood, theſe will be filled up by the Jelly, which, as it cools, will become very near as ſtiff as the other, and the Variety of Colour will ſhew the Shapes of the Moon and Stars very prettily.

It is one of the handſomeſt Diſhes that can be brought to a Table, and is excellent in its Kind.

6. *The floating Iſland.*

This is a very elegant Diſh, in which the Appearance is to be conſulted, the Eye being extremely pleaſed with it when well made, as well as the Palate.

Mix together a Quart of fine thick freſh Cream with a quarter of a Pint of Sack, and two large Spoonfuls of treble-refined Sugar powdered; grate in ſome Lemon Peel very fine, and mill this all together till it comes to a fine Froth.

Set a large China Diſh upon the Table, and ſet in this a Glaſs Diſh of ſuch a Size as to ſtand conveniently within it.

Pour away the thin from under the Froth into this Glaſs Diſh.

Cut the Crumb of two French Rolls into thin Slices, and lay them evenly as poſſible upon the Cream in the Glaſs Diſh.

Upon theſe put Currant Jelly to cover them entirely, but not to lie very thick upon them.

On the Currant Jelly lay another Layer of very thin Slices of Bread, and upon that lay ſome Hartſhorn Jelly, in the ſame Manner as the Currant Jelly was laid on the former.

Upon this lay another Covering of thin Slices of Bread, and upon that the Froth of the Cream well milled, and let it riſe as nigh as it can.

This

This done, lay Sweetmeats round the Edge of the Difh.

The whole Mafs will hold tolerably well together, and will move about upon the Cream in the Glafs Difh.

SECT. IV.

Of PICKLING.

THE Seafon of the Year is not yet come for doing a great deal in this Way, but as we fhall-advife the accomplifhed Houfekeeper to feize every Opportunity of adding to her Store-room, and of keeping her Hand in Ufe, we fhall find her fome Employment in this early Month, and enough in the following.

ART. I. *Pickled French Beans.*

French Beans make a very pleafant Pickle, and one that is very agreeable to the Eye. They never have fo good a Colour as when they are done young, therefore this is a Seafon for doing them finely.

Get a Peck of thofe fine, young, and tender French Beans, that are to be had at this Time of the Year, throw them into four or five Pans of cold Water one after another, ftirring them about with the Hand, that they may be perfectly clean.

Then cut off both Ends, and ftring them, but do not fplit or cut them any Way befide.

When they are thus prepared put them into a Stone Jar, and pour upon them as much Brine as will cover them: This Brine muft be made of very clear Water, by putting into it as much Salt as will make it bear an Egg; this muft be boiled up once, and then ftrained through a Flannel Bag, and poured upon the Beans hot.

Tie

Tie down the Jar, and let them ſtand thus four and twenty Hours.

Then take them out, ſtrain off the Brine, and dry the Beans between two Cloths.

Wipe out the Jar, and put into it ſome young Fennel, then put in the Beans again, and prepare the Pickle thus:

Mix together three Quarts of good Vinegar and one Quart of Spring Water, or ſo in Proportion for any Quantity that ſhall be ſufficient to cover the Beans; put in ſome Bay Salt to give it a Reliſh.

To a Gallon of the Pickle put a Nutmeg cut into Quarters, four Blades of Mace, a quarter of an Ounce of Cloves, a Spoonful of whole Pepper, and a couple of Races of Ginger ſhred; boil theſe up together in an earthen Pipkin, and pour them boiling hot upon the French Beans in the Jar; cover this up, and let it ſtand thus two Days.

At the End of that Time pour off the Pickle into a Pipkin, and boil it once up; when it boils pour it into the Jar again upon the Beans, and two Days afterward do this again; let them now ſtand till they are perfectly cold, and then cover them over with a Bladder well tied down, and over that with a Leather, which muſt be tied down carefully alſo. This compleats them, and they will be very delicate.

2. *Pickled Lemons.*

Chuſe half a dozen fine middle-ſized Lemons, freſh and perfectly ſound, ſcrape the Outſides of them with a Piece of a broken Quart Bottle, and then cut them lengthwiſe down into four Quarters, but not quite aſunder; they muſt be left ſo as to hang juſt together.

Rub theſe over with Salt on the rough Outſide, and fill the Cuts with Salt in the ſame Manner; put them into an earthen Diſh that will juſt hold them, ſprinkle ſome more Salt over them, and turn them once a Day; let them lie thus four Days.

Cut

Cut an Ounce of Ginger into thin Slices, and parboil twelve Cloves of Garlick, add to thefe a Handful
of Muftard-feed, and as much Cayon Pepper as will
lie upon a Shilling; fprinkle fome Salt among thefe,
and let them ftand all the Time the Lemons are in
the Pan.

Then have a clean Stone Jar ready, take out the
Lemons one by one, fqueeze them a very little, and
lay them carefully in the Jar; lay in the Spices all
about them and among them, pour in as much of
the beft white Wine Vinegar as will thoroughly cover
them, and tie them clofe down; let them ftand
a Month, and they will be fit to eat.

This is a very particular Pickle, but there are fome
People very fond of it.

SECT. V.
Of DISTILLERY.

WE have in general directed the Houfekeeper
in fuch a Manner in the Management of the
Stills of various Kinds, that fhe will not be at a Lofs
to make the very niceft, richeft, or fineft Waters that
can be ordered. Nothing is more creditable to keep
in a Family, and nothing more ferviceable; we fhall
therefore add here fome Receipts for the principal of
them, from approved Trials and repeated Practice.

ART. I. *Lady Allen's Water.*

Take Senicle, Scalions, Saint John's Wafh, and
Mugwort; Tormentil Roots and Leaves, Vervain,
Betony, and Celandine; Dragons Rofa Solis, Rofemary, Rhue, Mint, Balm, and Sage; Angelica, Mary-
goids, Columbines, Wormwood, Borage, Pimpernel,
Spleenwort, Burnet, Agrimony, and Carduus, of
each

each two Ounces, cut them all very fine, and chop and mix them together.

Mix together a Gallon of Milk and a Quart of white Wine, turn it thoroughly, then take off the Curd, and put the Whey into a Still.

Put in the Herbs, and ftir them all well together; let it heat gradually till it is juft ready to boil, taking off the Head of the Still, and frequently ftirring all about; then pour in a Quart of Brandy, and faften down the Head of the Still. Draw off two Quarts.

This is an excellent Cordial, and fweet. Let the Patient take a Glafs of it going to Bed when he has a Cold, and cover himfelf warm; it will throw him into a Sweat, and prevent a Fever.

A fmall Glafs of it is alfo very good for any one who is going into any Place where he fufpects there is a bad Air.

2. *Lady Hewet's Water.*

This is made of Lady Allen's Water, with the Addition of feveral excellent Ingredients, without any frefh Diftillation. Thefe Waters were fo much efteemed that many People who could not get the right Receipts made them at their own Pleafure, and called them by thefe excellent Ladies Names; but the true Receipts are given here. They are taken from the Family Book in Lady Hewet's own Hand Writing, which cannot be liable to any Miftake *. The Receipt is this:

Put into a Quart of Lady Allen's Water twelve Grains of Mufk, ten Grains of Ambergreafe, and fifteen Grains of Bezoar finely rubbed together in a Mortar, then put in one Dram of prepared Coral, one Dram of the Flower of Pearl, and half a Dram of the Flower of Amber; add half a Pound of white Sugarcandy beaten to Powder, four Leaves of Gold,

---

* This Book being purchafed among Mrs. Bradley's Papers, is now in the Hands of the Publifher, where the Curious may fee it.

and forty Grains of Saffron; fhake all this well together, and ftop it clofe.

This is as high a Cordial as it is poffible for the
Art of Man to make; it is a powerful Sweat, and is
good in Convulfions, and in rhumatick Fevers; one
Dofe of it, which is two large Spoonfuls, will frequently cure a Fever; it occafions a plentiful Sweat,
after which the Patient falls into an eafy Sleep, and
when he wakes he finds himfelf refrefhed in fuch a
Manner as is hardly to be conceived.

3. *Red Poppy, or Surfeit Water.*

Pick very clean half a Bufhel of frefh-gathered red
Poppy Flowers, and put them into three Gallons of
fine French Brandy, cover up the Pan into which
they are put, and let them ftand two Days and two
Nights fteeping, then ftrain off the Liquor.

Put into this Liquor two Pounds of Figgs cut into
thin Slices, and two Pounds of Raifins of the Sun
ftoned and chopped, add to thefe four Ounces of
frefh Liquorice Root fcraped clean, and then beaten
out into Threads, three Ounces of Annifeed beaten
fmall, and half a Pound of brown Sugar-candy.

Shake all well together, and fet them in the Sun
for fix Days, then ftrain off the Liquor, and bottle
it up for Ufe.

This is a very rich Tincture of Poppies rather than
a Water, for it is not diftilled; but as it is ufually
called red Surfeit Water, and is much efteemed in
Families, we thought it proper to give the Receipt in
this Place, which is alfo taken from the Lady Hewit's
Book. It is a Cordial and a Sweat: A Glafs of it
drank at any Time when a Perfon is difordered by a
Cold, or has an Oppreffion at the Stomach, is very
fine: It is alfo good againft a Pain in the Side, and
to throw out the Meafles, or Small Pox, or any other
Eruption; but then it muft be given in fmall Dofes,
and often repeated.

In

In thefe laft Cafes two Spoonfuls fhould be given at a Time, and the Perfon keep in Bed and favour the Sweat whereinto this Medicine will be fure to throw him.

It may in the fame Manner be given to Children, but then a Tea Spoonful is a Dofe, and it is a very fafe Medicine.

4. *Royal Water.*

Take Scordium, Carduus, Gumander, and Goats-rhue, of each two Handfuls; Citron and Orange Peel dried, of each two Ounces; if Citron Peel cannot be had Lemon Peel will do as well; the Seeds of Citron or Lemon, of Carduus and of Hartwort, and the Flowers of Marygolds and Rofemary, of each one Handful; cut the Herbs fmall, and pound the other Ingredients in a Mortar till they come to a Sort of coarfe Powder; put them into a Glafs Veffel, and pour upon them a Quart of Carduus Water and a Gallon of Brandy; fet it in the Sun for a Fortnight, well ftopped up, and fhake it frequently, then put it into the Still, and draw off a Gallon.

This is a very fine Cordial, and is good for Sick-nefs of the Stomach and Giddinefs in the Head; it alfo operates as a Sweat, and by that Means will fre-quently cure a Fever in the firft coming on before it has got to a Head.

5. *Snail Water.*

Put into a Still four Gallons of French Brandy; cut to Pieces the following Ingredients: Celandine, Betony, Agrimony, Woad, Bearsfoot, Rofemary, Angelica, Dragons and Barberry Bark, of each two Handfuls.

Put thefe into the Still, and ftir them thoroughly about with the Brandy; then add Burdock Root an Ounce, Cloves an Ounce, Turmerick an Ounce, and Saffron a quarter of an Ounce; let thefe be fliced and bruifed together, and put to the reft in the Still, once more ftiring all well about.

3 A 2   Then

Then put in half a Pound of Hartſhorn Shavings, a Peck of Snails, a Quart of Worms, and half a Peck of Wood Sorrel.

Put in a Gallon of Water, ſtir all well about again, and draw off four Gallons of the Water. It is a great Cordial.

6. *Lemon Water.*

Put a Gallon of French Brandy into a large, wide-mouthed Glaſs, and put into it the Rinds of twelve fine Lemons, and ſhake it up together; ſtop up the Veſſel, and ſhake them well again; let them ſtand two Days, frequently ſhaking the Glaſs, and then pour them into the Still; add a Quart of Water, and ſix Grains of Muſk tied up in a Piece of Muſlin.

Diſtil a Gallon, and put in three Ounces of powdered white Sugar-candy, with a quarter of a Pint of Roſe Water, and the ſame of Orange-Flower Water.

This is a very pleaſant Cordial, and ſtrengthens the Stomach.

7. *Aqua Silenæ.*

Take Cloves and Nutmegs of each an Ounce, Cinnamon and Jamaica Pepper of each two Ounces; put theſe into a Mortar, and bruiſe them thoroughly: Put into a Still three Gallons of Brandy, put in two Quarts of Water, and draw off three Gallons.

Sweeten this with two Pounds and a half of the fineſt Sugar, and tinge it with Cochineal to a fine crimſon.

Saunders Wood may be uſed inſtead of Cochineal, but it is not ſo well.

This is the plain Aqua Silenæ. It is a fine Cordial, much of the Nature of the Aqua Mirabilis kept by the Apothecaries. We ſhall ſhew in the next Receipt how it is to be made the rich Way.

8. *Rich Aqua Silenæ.*

Diſtil the plain Aqua Silenæ as ordered in the foregoing Receipt, and add to it, beſides the Sugar and

Cochi-

Cochineal, two Drams of Effence of Ambergreafe, and half an Ounce of the fineft Saffron.

Some make their rich Aqua Silenæ by putting thefe Ingredients into the Still with the reft, but they have ten Times the Effect when they are added afterwards, and the Saffron alfo enriches the Colour.

This Way made it is an excellent Cordial, good in Lownefs of Spirits, and as a Sweat in Fevers.

SECT. VI.

Remedies for various Difeafes.

ART. I. *For a four Humour on the Stomach.*

TAKE fine white Chalk an Ounce, the fineft Sugar three quarters of an Ounce, let thefe be rubbed to Powder, and add to them two Drams of Powder of Gum Arabick ; when all thefe are well rubbed together put them to a Quart of Water in a large Bottle, and fhake it well up.

The Dofe is a large Spoonful at a Time.

It cures the Heartburn, and it is good in Coughs rifing from a fharp, tickling Rheum.

If one Dofe does not cure the Heartburn let the Patient take another, and fo go on till he is well.

When Affes Milk curdles upon a Perfon's Stomach, a little of this put into it is fure to prevent that Accident ; and it mixes very well with it, without giving it any bad Tafte.

There is no Way fo good to give Chalk ; and the fitteft for this Ufe is what the Druggifts keep levigated in little Lumps, or elfe what is taken out of the Chalk Eggs found in the Chalk Pits of Kent and other Places.

Thefe

Thefe are Sea Hedgehog Shells full of Chalk, of the Bignefs of a large Egg; and the Chalk that is in them is always of the fineft Kind, and perfectly pure.

2. For *Hyfterick Fits.*

Put twelve Grains of Mufk in a Mortar, and grind it well with a quarter of an Ounce of the fineft powdered Sugar.

Take half a Pint of Damafk Rofe Water, and mix it by Degrees with the Mufk and Sugar. When all is well mixed it is fit for taking.

Some put only a Gill and half of Rofe Water to this Quantity, but upon Trial that is too ftrong.

A Wine Glafs of this is to be given at a Time in Hyfterick Fits.

When the Complaint is removed, a good Glafs of it fhould be taken to prevent Returns.

3. For *Difficulty of breathing.*

Pick out fome very fine and clean Gum Armoniacum, beat an Ounce and half of it to fine Powder, and grind it well with a little Hyffop Water; add more till there is a Quart got in, and then pour it out of the Mortar into a large Bottle, leaving the thickeft of the Settlement behind; add to this an Ounce of Oxymel of Squills, and half an Ounce of the Afthmatick Elixir.

This is excellent againft all Difficulties of breathing. It cuts tough Phlegm, and nothing is more ufeful to fuch as are hufky in a Morning.

It is famous in Afthmas, and in all Cafes where the Paffages are obftructed with a tough Phlegm.

The Dofe is two Spoonfuls going to Bed and early in the Morning.

4. For *Nervous Diforders in general.*

Take Pennyroyal Water four Ounces, Hyfterick Water two Ounces, Tincture of Caftor two Drams, volatile Salt of Hartfhorn ten Grains, white Sugar fix Drams; mix all together.

It

It is good in all Hyfterick and Nervous Cafes. The Dofe is a fmall Wine Glafs, and it may be repeated two or three Times a Day, as there is Occafion. It is good againft Obftructions, and anfwers excellently in thofe Diforders to which many Women are fubject from thofe Complaints.

5. *Againft Faintings.*

Take Milk Water four Ounces, Plague Water two Ounces, Tincture of Saffron and Sal Volatile Oleofum of each two Drams, and fine Sugar in Powder half an Ounce.

The Dofe of this is three Spoonfuls, and it is of excellent Service in Fevers, where the Spirits are low, and the Patient is weak and fainting. It anfwers excellently alfo in any occafional Faintnefs and Diforders of the Head.

6. *Againft Purgings in Fevers.*

Put into a Saucepan an Ounce of burnt Hartfhorn and three Pints of Spring Water, boil this to a Quart, pour it off, and add to it Cinnamon Water an Ounce, Sugar two Drams; fhake all well together.

This is very ufeful when Purgings come on in Fevers, and may be drank a quarter of a Pint at a Time warm, at Difcretion. When there is Occafion to have it ftronger, the following may be given in the fame Manner, but Care muft be taken left this check too fuddenly.

7. *Againft violent Purgings.*

Boil Hartfhorn and Water as in the former Receipt, and when it is done add to the Quart half an Ounce of Diafcordium made without Honey.

Let the Patient take four Spoonfuls of this three Times in the Day, always taking it juft after a Stool, till it abates.

8. *Againft*

8. *Againſt Spitting of Blood.*

Take Comfrey Root and Eryngo Root of each half an Ounce, Spring Water three Pints ; boil this well ; when it has boiled ſome Time put in two Ounces of Conſerve of red Roſes, and boil it till there is a Quart left, ſtrain this off, and drop in forty Drops of ſweet Spirit of Vitriol.

A Gill of this is to be drank twice a Day.

Beſide being excellent againſt Spitting of Blood, it is very ſerviceable to allay the Heat and Thirſt in Hectick Fevers, and is a very good Medicine in Conſumptions, when they are not advanced too far. It is beſt, when the Patient is in a very weak Way, to take it warm.

9. *Againſt the Gravel.*

Cut into thin Slices two Ounces of Burdock Root, boil it in three Pints of Water to a Quart, and then ſtrain it off ; add a Dram of vitriolated Tartar, and two Ounces of Syrup of Marſh-mallows.

This is to be taken a quarter of a Pint at a Time twice or three Times a Day, and it is an excellent and powerful Medicine.

Beſide bringing away Gravel and ſmall Stones, it is excellent in the Rheumatiſm, and will do great Service in the Gout.

'Tis alſo good againſt Spitting of Blood.

10. *A Clyſter for the Bloody-Flux.*

Make ſome ſtrong Starch, ſuch as is uſed in Waſhing, take four Ounces of this warm, and mix with it half an Ounce of Linſeed Oil cold drawn, and twenty-five Drops of Liquid Laudanum. Give it as a Clyſter, and let it be repeated if there be Occaſion, but not oftener than once in a Day.

It is of excellent Service not only in Bloody-fluxes, but in all ſharp Humours that happen to fall upon the Bowels ; it ſoftens, heals, and takes off the Pain in a Manner almoſt miraculous.

11. *For*

11. *For the Jaundice.*

Take a Handful of great Celandine Leaves and Roots, an Ounce of Turmerick, and an Ounce of Madder; put thefe into three Pints of Water, and boil them to a Quart.

Strain this off, and let it ftand to be cold.

Bruife two hundred Millepedes or Wood-Lice, and fqueeze out their Juice, put this to the Decoction, and add two Ounces of Syrup of Marfhmallows.

A quarter of a Pint of this is to be taken twice a Day till the Perfon is cured; for this very feldom fails of Succefs.

12. *Againft the Rheumatifm.*

Take Rafpings of Guiacum Wood two Ounces, Raifins of the Sun ftoned an Ounce and half, Spring Water three Quarts; boil it to three Pints; toward the End of the boiling add an Ounce of Saffafras Shavings, and half an Ounce of Liquorice Root beaten; when it has boiled fome Time with thefe take it off, let it ftand till cold, and then ftrain off the Liquor.

This fhould be taken half a Pint at a Time, twice a Day, for a confiderable Time. It fweetens the Blood, and operates by Sweat and Urine. It was at one Time efteemed a fovereign Remedy for the Venereal Difeafe, but at prefent we have more efficacious and fpeedy Remedies.

13. *Againft Coughs.*

Put into three Quarts of Water an Ounce of French Barley and an Ounce of ftoned Raifins, four good Figs, and half an Ounce of Liquorice Root beaten; boil this to two Quarts, and, toward the End of the Time when it is boiling, add half an Ounce of the Root of Florentine Orrice, and of the Leaves of Harts Tongue and the Flowers of Coltsfoot each an Ounce; when the boiling is finifhed ftrain it off, and let the Patient take a quarter of a Pint of it warm three Times a Day.

It foftens fharp Humours, and gives great Relief in Coughs of all Kinds.

It is alfo ferviceable in the Gravel and in Pleurifies.

It may be given very properly alfo in the Small Pox and Meafles; foftening the Mouth and Throat, and throwing out the Eruptions.

14. *Againſt a Dropſy.*

Cut into thin Slices an Ounce of the Sennekka Rattlefnake Root, boil it in a Pint and half of Water to a Pint, and add to this an Ounce of Syrup of Marfhmallows.

Let the Patient drink a Wine Glafs of this twice a Day.

It works very powerfully by Urine, and is excellent in the Beginning of a Dropfy, as alfo in Pleurifies, and many other Diforders.

The Root from which it is made is to be had at the Druggifts. It has but lately been brought into Ufe in Phyfick in England, and it feems now in a Way to be neglected, though a good Drug.

15. *For inward Bruiſes.*

Take of Ground Ivy Leaves picked from the Stalks, and of Plantain Leaves, each half an Ounce, Spring Water three Pints, boil it away to a Quart, and then add an Ounce of white Sugar.

The Patient is to take a quarter of a Pint three Times a Day warmed.

It is very healing, and fomewhat reftringent, fo that it will ftop inward Bleedings.

SECT.

S E C T. VII.

Of the Diforders of Cattle, and their Remedies.

THESE we fhall here, as in the preceding Months, arrange under feveral Heads, according to the Creatures fubject to them, and fhall lay down nothing as a Cure for which we have not Experience and Practice.

C H A P. I.

Of the Horfe.

WE fhall under this Head confider the great Importance of this Animal for Ufe as well as Pleafure, and treat of his feveral Diforders, from the moft common and eafy of Cure to the moft difficult and rare; in all Cafes paying Regard only to fuch Remedies as have been tried by the moft judicious Farriers, and found fuccefsful.

ART. I. *For a Horfe that is fick at the Stomach.*

A Glut of Provender, or fome new Kind to which a Horfe is not ufed, will often take an Effect upon his Stomach of very dangerous Tendency : This will be firft feen in his loathing his Food, and afterwards by his cafting up his newly-eaten Meat by the Way of vomiting.

A Change of Water will fometimes occafion the fame Accident alfo.

The firft Thing to be examined is, which of thefe is the Caufe ; and which foever it prove to be, that

muft

muft be removed before there can be any Hope of Succefs from Medicines of any Kind; becaufe if the Creature went on in the Way that occafioned his Diforder, his Food and Drink would be renewing it as faft as the Medicines could cure it.

When he is brought to his ufual Diet and Drink, one of the two following will prove a certain Remedy.

Mix half an Ounce of Diapente in a Quart of good Ale, and give it to him warm; repeat this every Morning for three Days, and be careful that he have the beft Hay and other Provifions.

If this do not reftore him, put an Ounce of Salt of Tartar into a Pint and half of Vinegar, and when it is diffolved add to it a Quart of Mint Water; divide this into four Parts, and give him one every Morning and Evening.

During the taking of this Medicine he muft be fed with Moderation from the Hand, and in the following Manner:

He muft be kept fafting an Hour before and three quarters of an Hour after the Medicine; then give him a good Piece of Bread, and after that a Lock of very fweet and fine Hay; and let his Drink be the pureft River Water a little warmed.

Thus he is to be fed carefully and fparingly, and while he is not eating a Bag is to be hung at his Nofe, in which is to be put a large Piece of brown Bread fopp'd in Vinegar; the Vapour of this will ftrengthen his Stomach and affift the Power of the Medicines.

Thus he will certainly be cured, and he muft be fed with more Care than ufual to prevent a Relapfe.

2. *Of the Hungry Evil.*

This is a Diforder juft the contrary of the former; it is common to our own Species as well as to this Creature. In Men it is called a Canine Appetite.

When a Horfe has this Diforder he eats a monftrous Quantity of Food, and it does him no good.

He

He will be found to have it by his violently fnatch-
ing at his Meat, and greedily fwallowing it without
chewing.

The Cure is this: Boil a Gallon of Milk and let
it ftand to be near cold, then ftir in a Pint of fine
Flour and a Quart of Sallad Oil; divide this into
four Dofes, and give him one every Morning.

After he has taken the Medicine, directly offer him
Food, and he will not be fo fond of it.

If this does not fucceed the fame Medicine muft be
given twice a Day, and then it very rarely fails. It
is in that Cafe to be given in the following Manner:
One Dofe is to be given as before directed in the
Morning, and he is to have fome Meat juft after it;
then he is to be kept without any Food five Hours;
in this Time he will grow very hungry; and then,
inftead of giving him Food he muft have another
Dofe of the Medicine; juft after that he is to be of-
fered Food again, and repeating this for three, four,
or five Days, will certainly cure him.

After this he muft be watched, for it is a very
natural Thing for him to relapfe; and when the leaft
Tendency to that is obferved he muft have one Dofe
more of the Medicine, which feldom fails to prove a
final Cure for the Diforder.

3. *Of Obftrufrom in the Liver.*

Horfes are very fubject to Obftructions in the
Liver, which make them pine and grow thin, and
afterwards fwell, and in the End are mortal.

The Diforder is known by the Horfe's looking
poor, his Eyes at Times yellow, and his Head continually turned in a moanful Way to the Body.

In this Cafe his Water is to be tinctured in the
following Manner: Boil a Pound of long Birthwort
Root and half a Pound of Turmerick, both bruifed
in a Mortar, in a Pot full of Water till there is but
a Gallon left, ftrain this off, and put a little of it
into his Water at firft, afterwards increafe the Quantity,

tity, for being ufed to the Tafte by Degrees he will bear it at laft to be very ftrong, and yet drink it freely; this is to be continued till he is well, and the ftronger his Water is made with it the fooner that will be.

4. *Of Purging and Bloody-Flux.*

This is a Diforder into which Horfes fall from bad Water and four Food, and fometimes from too hard Labour; it begins with the Stools being very thin, and as it continues they grow bloody, and at laft, if proper Care be not taken, the Horfe will void in a manner clear Blood.

The Remedy is this: Gather a large Quantity of Yarrow, the fame of Shepherds Purfe, and a Pound of Comfry Roots; boil thefe, being firft chopped fmall, in two Gallons of Water to a Gallon, prefs this out hard, and divide it into four Dofes; give him one of them warm, with a quarter of a Pint of red Wine, every Morning, and let him eat a good Quantity of Beans among his Food.

If this fail after three Dofes, make fuch another Quantity, and boil among it three quarters of an Ounce of Roach Allum. Give this as the other.

C H A P. II.

Of Oxen and Cows.

A R T. I.   *Of Cattle's declining their Food.*

OXEN and Cows, as well as Horfes, will fome-times take a Diflike to their Food, and in con-fequence they will grow thin, fickly, and weak, and their Hair will often fall off in great Quantities, and what remains on will change Colour.

In this Cafe give the following Medicine:

Pound in a Mortar four Ounces of Shavings of Ivory, add to it three quarters of an Ounce of Myrrh

in

in Powder, and when thefe are well mixed, work them up with as much Butter as will be fufficient to make the whole into a Pafte; divide this into three Lumps, roll them up as Balls, and give one of them every third Morning, giving after it a Pint of warm Mint Water, with a Gill of red Wine and a Lump of Sugar.

2. Of Cattle that are Hide-bound.

Large Oxen, in Countries where they work them inftead of Horfes, are very fubjeĉt to this Complaint from over Labour, and in other Places they fometimes fall into it from Negleĉt or bad Pafture.

Whichfoever be the Occafion, the Remedy is this:

Let the Ox be firft blooded.

Then mix together half an Ounce of Bay-Berries in Powder, and a quarter of an Ounce of Powder of Myrrh, brew thefe up in a Quart of warm Ale, and give it to the Beaft every other Morning; let him be kept quiet, and fed with good Hay, and after four Dofes of the Medicine let him be turned into a good Pafture.

His Skin will foon grow loofe, and he will get into Flefh, and thrive.

3. Of Diforders of the Lungs.

Oxen and Cows are fubjeĉt to Diforders of the Lungs as well as human Creatures, and they generally arife from the fame Caufe, fudden Cold after violent heating.

A Beaft is known to be thus difordered by its panting, breathing hard, or coughing.

The Remedy is this: Take a Pint of Tanners Ooze, a Quart of new Milk, and a quarter of a Pint of Sallad Oil, diffolve in thefe an Ounce and half of brown Sugar-candy, and give it to the Creature in a Morning before it eats any Thing, for three Days; upon the third Day give before it a Ball of Tar and

Butter;

Butter; keep the Creature warm, and it generally makes a complete Cure, and without much Danger of a Return.

C H A P. III.

Of Sheep.

A R T. I. *Of the Red-water.*

THIS is a very fatal Difeafe to Sheep, but if taken in Time it is not difficult to cure.

Firft let the Sheep that have it be feparated from the others, and then let each of them be blooded pretty largely; then give the following Medicine:

Bruife fome Rhue and Wormwood, equal Quantities of each, and to fo much of thefe Ingredients as will yield a Quart of Juice add a large Handful of live Wood-lice.

Squeeze all ftrongly out, and give half a Pint at a Time for four Days, in the Morning.

The bleeding fhould be in two Places, between the Hoofs and under the Tail.

2. *Of the Pimple Evil.*

This is a Diforder in Sheep, which confifts in a great Multitude of red Pimples rifing on the Skin. It is alfo called the Pox.

It is an infectious Diforder, and therefore the firft Thing to be done is to feparate the Sheep that are afflicted with it from the reft, that it do not fpread among the Flock.

The Cure is this: Boil the Roots of Milkwort in Water, and add fome Milk to it.

Give half a Pint of a pretty ftrong Decoction of this every Morning.

Cut a good Quantity of Rofemary Tops, and boil them in Vinegar till the Vinegar is very ftrong of them; then wafh all the Places where the Pimples

are

are with this two or three Days together; when this Courfe is over turn out the Sheep into a Pafture, and they will be well, and may mix with the others in a Week.

S E C T. VIII.

Of the Management of a Garden and Orchard.

THIS is not quite fo bufy a Month as the laft for the Garden, but a great deal may be done in it. We fhall in this, as in the preceding Months, feparate the Work under three Heads, as it regards Trees, eatable Plants, and Flowers, and fhall give the Reader under each Head his proper and full Directions.

C H A P. I.

Of Trees.

THE Gardiner now is to put the laft Hand to his Fruit Trees to prepare them for the Summer's Service. The pruning and nailing, if any Part of it be defective, muft be fupplied and finifhed, and this muft be done where needful with a very tender Hand, for it is a Seafon too far advanced for fuch Operations.

Let him now, for the laft Time, look carefully over his Trees, and fee if there be any dead Wood that efcaped his Eye before; if he find any, let it not ftand to burden the Tree and difgrace his Care, but let him with a fharp Knife and a fteady Hand cut it out.

All that is required now for thefe is to have them undifturbed; let him guard them from Injuries, and feaft his Eye with the daily Obfervation of the Fruits Nature is preparing.

For fuch Trees as have been planted this Spring, or the Autumn before, fome Care is required, that they do not fuffer by the growing Heat.

If the Seafon be dry they muft be fometimes watered, if not there needs none of this Trouble, Nature doing the Bufinefs much better than Men can.

Let a Heap of Stones be laid round the Bottom of every new planted Tree: This anfwers two Purpofes; the one is keeping the Earth moift about the Roots, and the other is keeping the Tree fteady.

Some content themfelves with laying Weeds or Straw about the Roots, but this anfwers only half the Purpofe, and that but imperfectly.

Let the careful Gardiner watch the Shoots of his new-planted Trees, and rub off fuch as grow ill, that the reft which have a better Direction may flourifh the more.

Cherry Trees that are in Danger of being Hidebound are now to be eafed, by flitting down the Bark in fuch Places with a Knife. It is remarkable that the Grain of Cherry Bark runs circularly, fo that this Method is fure to relieve them.

Let the Vines be watched this Month, and all the ufelefs Shoots removed; and the Suckers be taken from the Roots of Fig Trees.

This will be all required for the Care of Trees.

C H A P. II.

Of Plants.

LET the Gardiner now clean his Allies, and lay all in Order in his Kitchen Garden.

Let

Let him fow Beets, Sorrel, Parfley, Onions, and Chibols, and defend his Seed Onions from the Wind, which at this Seafon will be apt elfe to break them, the Stalks being weak and the Heads heavy.

This is a very good Time to fow French Beans.

Chufe for this Purpofe a dry Soil and a warm Border, and fow them in fhallow Trenches opened by a Line: The Seeds fhould be dropped in about four Inches afunder, and the Trenches opened about two Feet afunder.

Rouncival Peafe are to be fown at this Time, as alfo other Peafe and Beans for late Crops.

There is alfo another very good Practice for the providing a late Crop of Beans, which is, in fome Places where the Rows ftand thick, to cut down every other Row within three Inches of the Ground; this will give the other Rows Air, and make them thrive and bear abundantly; and there will in the mean Time rife a vaft Number of Shoots where the Stalks are cut, and thefe will be loaded with Beans late in the Autumn.

This is the beft Seafon for propagating Rofemary and Lavender, and the like Herbs, by Cuttings. Chufe a dry fhowery Seafon for this; and obferve that Cuttings of Rofemary fucceed this Way juft as well as Slips, and do not hurt the Mother Plant in taking off, whereas the Slips tear and make Wounds that do not eafily heal; many a fine Shrub of Rofemary has died from this the next Winter, when the Caufe was forgot, and the Damage laid only to Frofts.

There is no Seafon at which the Garden is fo over-run with Vermin, and every Method is now to be ufed to deftroy them,

This Month Lettuces fhould be fown to fucceed the former Crops, and Purflain and Nafturtium fhould be fown to take their Chance in the naked Ground.

Take Care of the Strawberry Beds at this Seafon, and if it be dry let them be well watered once in three

Days;

Days : The Fruit will come in fuch Abundance as very well to repay the Trouble.

Young Salleting fhould be fown now as ufual, and fome Celeri may very well be fown in the natural Ground, or, what will anfwer better, on a decayed Hot-Bed.

Chardoons are now to be fown in the natural Earth, and the beft Way is this: Place four Seeds in a Hole made with a Stick, and make thefe Holes at five Feet Diftance.

When the young Plants come up obferve which is the ftrongeft, and pull up all the reft in each Hole; only one is to be left in each, which is then to ftand for blanching.

The Beds of Carrots and Parfnips are now to be hoed, to deftroy the Weeds and thin the Plants ; they fhould now be left at about eight Inches Diftance. The Beds of Onions are alfo to be hoed with the fame Intent, and thefe are to be left at about four Inches.

Ridges are now to be made for Cucumbers and Melons for a full Crop, and the fuperfluous Branches from the Melon Plants are to be cut off from the forward Ridge. In making of thefe Ridges, if the Ground be dry the Dung fhould be but little higher than the Surface, and Earth is to be laid upon the Dung to the Thicknefs of a Foot and half.

This is not the proper Practice where the Ground is cold and damp ; the Dung muft be there raifed higher above the Surface, otherwife the whole will come to nothing, becaufe the Coldnefs and Wet of the Ground will deftroy all the Virtue of the Dung, its Heat will be loft, and the Plants perifh.

The young Celeri Plants are to be tranfplanted this Month into Beds of a deep rich Earth, and placed at about fix Inches Diftance; thefe muft be watered flightly till they have taken Root; if there be fcanty Room they may be fet at three Inches Diftance ; and the whole Seed Bed fhould not be cleared for this, but fome of the Plants left to thrive there.

The

The Ground muſt now be hoed between the Rows of Beans and Peaſe, and drawn up about the Stems of Cabbage and Cauliflower Plants.

In cold Nights Glaſſes muſt be put over Cucumbers and Melons, otherwiſe much of the young Fruit will drop off the Stalks.

C H A P. III.

Of Flowers.

THE Weeds grow very quick this Month, there-fore the Work of cleaning and hoeing the Borders muſt be repeated frequently.

Many of the taller Flowers will now be growing high in Stalk, and the Gardiner muſt from Time to Time go his Rounds, and tie them up to Sticks.

In this Month many of the annual Flowers are to be ſown, Lupines, Flos Adonis, Convolvulus, Catch-fly, and many other Kinds.

This is alſo the beſt Seaſon of the whole Year for ſowing of the hardy biennial Plants, ſuch as Canter-bury Bells, Columbines, Sweet Williams, and the like.

It is a very good Practice to make ſome ſlight hot Beds this Month for the raiſing of the annual Flowers, ſuch as the French and African Marygolds, and the like.

The common Practice is to ſow theſe earlier upon conſiderably ſtrong hot Beds, and under Frames and Glaſſes; but as they are to be removed young into the natural Earth, and to ſtand all the Seaſon, it is much better to raiſe them thus on Borders with a ſlighter Heat, and covered with Matts, for thus they are nearer a common Earth and free Air, and will be leſs checked by the Removal.

Several of the Seedlings on the hot Beds ſhould now be tranſplanted to other hot Beds made for their Re-ception.

It

It is a good Practice to put fome Tuberofe Roots in at this Time to fucceed the earlier. The Carnation Stalks fhould now be fupported by Sticks, for they are weak, and the Head forming they will be heavy, and in Danger of bowing down.

The Auriculas now begin to flower, and they muft be preferved from Wet, and from all other Injuries; 'tis proper therefore to place them upon their Stage under Cover.

Evergreens may yet be tranfplanted with Safety, and this is a good Time for cutting off their irregular Branches, that young ones may rife in their Places, either naturally, or by the Gardiner's Care and Direction: Though he may not be able to manage fuch as were grown ftubborn, he will eafily reduce thofe to proper Form which fhoot under his Eye, and fubmit themfelves to his Management while tender.

THE

A Dinner in May.

FIRST COURSE.

1. Turkey Poult:
2. Custards & Chickens
3. Tarts.
4. Green Goose.
5. Gooseberry Pye.
6. Cray Fish.
7. Leveret.

SECOND COURSE.

B. Cole sc.

THE

COOK, HOUSEKEEPER's,

AND

GARDINER's COMPANION.

M A Y.

SECT. I.

Provisions.

Bill of Fare for the Month of MAY.

THE Seafon of Plenty is advancing faft upon us, and every Month now will bring many Things of the Summer Produce to add to the Winter's Fare, and intermix with the more fubftantial Kinds.

ART. I. *For a firft Courfe.*

In general the Butcher's Shop holds the fame Appearance, and fupplies us with the fame repeated Fare; but of his fubftantial Provifion, fome Kinds and fome Joints being larger and heavier, are fitter for the Winter, fome lighter and more adapted to the Summer. This is all the Variety we find in the prefent Article; for Oxen do not fly away like Woodcocks, nor Sheep die off like the Produce of the Garden. The Houfekeeper is in general to form her Choice what Pieces to prefer in each Kind, according to the Direction juft laid down, of the larger for the colder

and

and the lighter for the warmer Weather; and we fhall
here affift her Memory by naming what Joints are
propereft at a handfome Table.

Beef is lefs efteemed in Summer; but when there
are large Companies, and the Table not intended to
be very expenfive, nothing is fo proper. In general
fmaller Pieces are preferable at this Time. The Rump
roafted, or fome good fmall Piece boiled, may come
on in a firft Courfe.

From the Ox Kind we are alfo to rekon the Tongue
and Udder, which may be fent up either roafted or
boiled with Cauliflower or Brocoli.

Veal is much better in Seafon than Beef; the Neck
roafted, or the Loin, or any other of the beft Joints,
are proper. The Breaft raggoo'd is alfo very proper;
and a Calf's Head any Way dreffed.

The Chine of Mutton roafted with Sallads or
Pickles; and any of the good Joints boiled with
Roots do very properly in a firft Courfe.

Bacon is of great ufe at this Time with Beans, and
on other Occafions.

As to Poultry, this is a Month in which many of
the Kinds of Fowls are not to be had, but the common Sorts are five: Chickens, grown Fowls, Capons,
and Paulards are in Perfection, and may be fent up
plain, or according to the feveral elegant Ways we
have defcribed.

Fifh are a very plentiful Refource for the Table at
this Seafon: Salmon and Smelts are in high Seafon,
and from our frefh Water Ponds we have Carp and
Tench in high Perfection, and from the Brooks and
Rivers Cray-fifh and Eels. The Carp or Tench
ftewed, and the Eels boiled or pitchcock'd, may be
fent up, or the Eel collar'd. Lobfters alfo are in
Seafon, but Oifters and moft other Shell-fifh out.

If to this Lift of Provifions we add the Pies and
Puddings furnifhed by the Paftry, there can be no
want of Variety for a firft Courfe.

2. *For*

2. *For a second Courfe.*

We have a large Supply alfo of Provifions, and many of them of the moft elegant Kind, for a fecond Courfe. Venifon is finely in Seafon, and 'tis a Time for Fawn, of which fome are very fond. Leverets alfo are fine now, and Kid, for thofe who approve it, may be had and dreffed as Fawn ; the beft Method for either of which is to have a Quarter roafted.

Of Poultry for a fecond Courfe we have all the young Kinds of the common and domeftick Breed. Turkey Pouts are very fine now, as are alfo Green Geefe and Ducklings : And of the wild Kind there are Quails.

Of the Fifh Kind there are fome of thofe already named that may be very well introduced in a fecond Courfe, as roafted Lobfter, collar'd Eel, Cray-fifh, and Prawns.

From the Paftry we may have many confiderable Articles ; a Variety of the Pie Kind, as alfo Tarts, Cuftards, Cheefecakes, and Creams.

We have thus, in the Account of Provifions in general for the fucceeding Month, given them under a Divifion ufual enough in other Books, but different from our general Method, that is according to the feveral Courfes in the which they are fitteft to appear. This has been done once by the Defire of fome who wifh no Article of Information fhould be wanting in this Work refpecting the Subject whereof it treats : By this Means the lefs experienced in thefe Things will fee which Difhes are proper for the firft and which for the fecond Service ; andthis may be feen in one Month as well as all, for all the other Kinds may be referred to thofe here named, or difpofed according to thefe general Directions : We fhall therefore in the Provifions for the fucceeding Months follow the former Rule of difpofing in our Bill of Fare all the Articles of each feveral Kind under its proper Head ; all the Meats under one Article, all the Fowls under another, and fo of the reft, this laying them before the Eye more diftinctly and with lefs Confufion, which we apprehend to be the Intent of an ufeful Bill of Fare. The Remainder of this Head comprehending the Garden Productions, whether Roots, Greens, or Fruits, we fhall treat all in this Manner.

Garden Stuff in Seafon in May.

This is a plentiful Month for the Provifions from the Garden, many coming continually into Seafon. The young Salleting of all Kinds is now in great Perfection ; it rifes quick from the fowing, by means of the increafing Warmth of the Weather, and it is a Rule in this Article, that the quicker the Leaves rife the tenderer they are.

Spinach is now in great Perfection, it never has its Colour, Juice, or Flavour finer.

There are alfo the Spring Coleworts and early Cabbages.

Afparagus is in the higheft Perfection ; and there is another Bud fit to be named on this Occafion, becaufe it is excellent in its Kind, and approaches to the Nature of the Afparagus in Delicacy, but being lefs common it will give an agreeable Variety, this is the Tragopogon or Garden Goatfbeard. We have mentioned the Hop Top or young Shoot of the Hop in a former Month, as being of the Nature of Afparagus ; that being now too rank, the Shoot of the Tragopogon follows it, and exceeds it in all Refpects ; it is larger, tenderer, and more juicy, and has a peculiar and very agreeable Tafte. This is to be dreffed in the fame Way as Afparagus ; but there is another Method we fhall lay down, which is a new Difh juft getting into ufe at fome great Tables, and is, though not expenfive, very elegant as well as very pleafant.

One Thing farther we fhall mention refpecting the Tragopogon Shoot, which is, that it is wholefome and nourifhing beyond moft Things which are the Produce of the Garden ; nothing that can be taken by Way of Food reftores decayed Nature like it.

Befides

Befides thefe already named, the Garden will now afford fome early Artichokes and Cauliflowers.

Thefe are the Greens in Seafon; as to Roots they are in general coming in: There will be fine early Turnips now ready for pulling, tender, and of a beautiful Colour. Radifhes are in their great Perfection, efpecially the fcarlet Radifh lately and juftly come into Fafhion; this is delicate and tender, of a fine lively Colour, and tranfparent, and has a better Flavour and lefs Heat than the common purple Radifh; there is alfo another Quality that may well recommend it, this is, it digefts more freely and is not fo apt to rife in the Stomach.

There will be in a good Garden young Carrots at this Time; they muft be fown in warm Borders for this Purpofe, and the Heat brings them forward, efpecially under a Wall; thefe have not the fine full Flavour of the Carrot that comes in fomewhat later, but they exceed all others in Colour.

Among the Fruit Products of the Kitchen Garden we are here to reckon French Beans, which now begin to come in from the Hot-Beds, as alfo Cucumbers, and fome early Melons.

The Houfekeeper is to give frequent Notice to the Gardiner of her expecting thefe Things, for they always pleafe particularly when they come fo early. In Town they come dear, becaufe they go through feveral Hands before they come to the Table, but in the Country the Charge is little, for nothing is cheaper than Labour.

Mufhrooms are another Article from the Beds in the Garden at this Time; and to this Lift we may add feveral Sorts of early Lettuces, Onions, Chives, Purflain, and the common favoury Herbs, Mint, Thyme, Balm, Winter Savoury, and the like.

Fruits in Seafon in May.

The latter End of May may be accounted the Earneft of the Year for Fruits; we have fcarce any

Thing

Thing thoroughly ripe in a natural Way at this Seafon indeed, but the Art and Affiftance of the Gardiner fhew us what we may expect from fuch Means : They foreftal the Productions of the natural Soil, and tho' what they offer are not equal to thofe which follow in their own Time, in Flavour, yet their being early is a great Recommendation.

There is a Cherry called the May Duke, and it is a very good one; it is the earlieft ripe of all, and with a little Affiftance of the Gardiner's forcing, comes in juft in Time to fave the Credit of its Name. A good Table need not be without this Cherry in May, and it is always extremely valued.

This Month we muft be content with the few we have, and be choice of them; the next will pour them upon us in great Plenty.

There is another Kind of this Fruit not called the May Duke, but plainly the May Cherry : It is faid by the Gardiners to come in fomewhat earlier than the May Duke, but the Difference is not effential, becaufe it is not certain or conftant.

Scarlet Strawberries begin to ripen at this Seafon, and if the Plants be examined in the warmft Borders, fome are ufually found.

Goofberries and green Currants are alfo juft coming in for Tarts.

There are two other Fruits very much efteemed at this Seafon, the Mafculine Apricot and the Nuting Peach; thefe owe their Ripenefs at that early Period to Art.

Befide thefe Fruits which are juft beginning to come in there are fome not quite gone out; thefe are a few Kinds of Apples and Pears.

Of the Apple Kind we often meet with the Golden and Winter Ruffet, as alfo Pile's Ruffet, and the Nonpareil, very good; but this muft have been owing to a very careful Manner of keeping them. The Stone Pippin, Oaken Pippin, and John Apple fometimes alfo laft good till now, and the Pomme d'Appi, which is a very good Kind.

The

The Pears to be had tolerably good at this Time are but few, the Beſſy de Chaumontelle is the principal; there are alſo the Amozelle, Bergamot, de Payne, and Lord Cheney's Green: Theſe are for the Deſert, and there are two that do for baking; theſe are the Cadillac and that Kind we call Perkinſon's Warden, but a careful Manner of preſerving is alſo requiſite for theſe.

S E C T. II.

Of C O O K E R Y.

C H A P. I.

Of Roaſting.

A R T. I. *To roaſt a Capon with ſweet Herbs.*

CHUSE a fine large Capon, let it be carefully picked and drawn, then raiſe the Skin from the Fleſh to looſen it.

Cut to Pieces a large Muſhroom, a Couple of Truffles, and ſhred ſome Parſley; mix theſe together; grate a quarter of a Pound of fine Bacon, mix this with the others; then cut very ſmall ſome Chives and ſome freſh and young Leaves of Garden Baſil, ſtrew over theſe ſome Pepper and Salt; then bruiſe half a Nutmeg, one Blade of Mace, and a couple of Cloves; ſtir this in, and when well mixed, the Stuffing is ready, put it carefully in between the Skin and Fleſh, and when it is well diſpoſed all over, ſew up the End, or tie it carefully, and then lard the Capon; this is to be done in a particular Manner. Some Ham muſt be cut into very thin Slices, and ſome Veal, and a good Quantity of ſweet Herbs, with ſome grated Nutmeg, is to be prepared and ſet ready.

The

The Capon is to be larded interchangeably with one Piece of Ham and another of Veal; and when this is done the fweet Herbs muft be ftrewed very thick over it.

Thus prepared the Capon is to be rolled up in two Sheets of Paper, and carefully roafted.

The Sauce may be a rich Gravy.

The French, who never know when to ftop, ferve up a Capon done in this Manner with a rich Raggoo about it, but this is Confufion, and the Tafte of one Thing deftroys that of another.

They who would be at the Top of the French Tafte may ferve it in this Manner, but with Gravy it is a very delicate and fine Difh, and no Way extravagant in the Expence.

2. *To roaft a Chicken with Ham.*

This is a Difh we owe to the French, and it is a very good one; not troublefome or expenfive. We allow that the Tafte of Ham and that of Chicken are very proper together, and we for that Reafon drefs them to be eat together, though they come to Table feparate. The French fend up all in one, and that in a much more agreeable Manner.

Chufe a fine well-grown Chicken, let it be truffed for roafting.

Cut a large fine Slice of Ham from the prime Part, Fat and Lean together; lay this on the Dreffer, beat it with a Knife to bruife but not break it, and ftrew upon it fome fhred Parfley, and a very fmall Quantity of Chives put among it.

When the Slice of Ham is feafoned, beat, and ready, loofen the Skin from the Breaft of the Chicken with a Finger, then get in the Slice of Ham thus prepared, and fee that it cover the whole Breaft, and lie very even between the Flefh and Skin.

Blanch the Chicken thus prepared before the Fire, and then wrap round it broad thin Slices of Bacon, tie thefe round with Packthread, and fpit the Chicken.

When

When the Chicken is roafted take off the Bacon, and ferve it up with fome Gravy or Effence of a Gammon of Bacon.

3. *To roaft a Gammon of Bacon.*

This, when properly roafted, makes an excellent Difh, but two Things are needful, the one to frefhen it, and the other to give it a Flavour. The beft Method is this:

Have fome luke-warm Water ready, a good Quantity, ftrip off the Skin carefully from a Gammon of Bacon, and when cleaned pour the warm Water over it; let it lie thus fome Time to take out the violent Saltnefs.

When taken out of the Water pour upon it in an earthen Pan a Quart of Sack, turn it, and let it lie twelve Hours in this Liquor.

When taken out of the Wine, fpit it and cover the fat Side of it with fome Sheets of white Paper.

Lay it to a good Fire, and pour all the Sack into the Dripping-pan; this is to bafte it, which muft be done from Time to Time all the while it is roafting.

When the Gammon is near done rub fome Bread to very fine Crumbs, and mix with it fome Parfley chopped very fine; take off the Papers, and ftrew the Gammon very well over with this, brown it up very well before a brifk Fire, and then take it off.

Some eat this hot, and it is that Way a pleafant Thing, but ftrong. The Spaniards, to whom we are obliged for this Piece of Cookery, only eat it cold. Their Way is this: They take it very carefully off the Spit not to rub away the Crumbs, and fet it to cool; when cold they lay a clean Napkin in a Difh and lay the Gammon upon it, garnifhing it with Parfley. It is this Way very fine, and much preferable to the eating it hot.

4. *To roaft a Quarter of Kid the French Way.*

Let the Kid be fmall and delicate, lard one half of the Quarter very well with fat Bacon, and having
grated

grated fome Crumbs of Bread very fine, with this lard the other half, then wrap it up in Paper, and lay it down at a moderate Diftance from a very good Fire.

Referve fome of the Bread Crumbs, and mix with them fome fhred Parfley and a little Salt. When the Kid is near done take off the Papers, and drudge that Part which was drudged at firft, very well with thefe Crumbs.

When this is done brifk up the Fire, and finifh it very brown ; fend it up hot, firft fqueezing half a fine Seville Orange over it, and garnifh it with Orange in thick Slices.

Many are very fond of Kid, but in general it is inferior to Lamb. If it be not very young it is apt to tafte rank ; and that which is bred in Towns among Stables, and in the Way of Filth, is never fo well flavoured as what is bred more naturally in the Country ; at the beft the Flefh is drier than Lamb, but when fine it has a very peculiar Sweetnefs.

5.　*To roaft Larks larded.*

Let the Larks be clean picked and truffed handfomely with the Feet on their Backs, then cut fome very thin and fine Pieces of Bacon for larding of them ; fpit them very carefully, and lay them down to roaft.

Mix together fome Crumbs of Bread and fome Bafket Salt. When the Larks are near enough drudge them with this, and then let them have a Turn or two more very near the Fire.

Warm the Difh, and rub a Shalot over it, but leave none of it in ; 'tis only to give a light Flavour. They are thus extremely good, eaten dry, which is now a great Tafte. Some make Bread Sauce for them in the ufual Way, and others make a Sauce of Orange Juice, Pepper, and Salt ; the French add to this a little Verjuice.

6. *Larks*

6. *Larks barded.*

The French Cooks brought in this Term Barded; they call a thin flat Slice of Bacon fit to wrap round any Thing a Bard of Bacon, and any Thing that is dreſſed this Way they call barded. Thus Larks are to be barded in the following Manner :

Let the Larks be truſſed in the ſame Way as before directed, and cut for every one of them a thin Slice of Bacon broader and longer than the Lark; ſpit them upon a wooden Skewer, with one of theſe Bards or Pieces of Bacon between every two, and when they are near roaſted drudge them with Bread and Salt.

When they are enough take them up, place them regularly on a Diſh, and ſend up Bread Sauce if in the Engliſh Way, but if the French it is to be very fine Juice of Orange and Juice of Lemon, of each equal Parts, and a good deal of Pepper and Salt in it. We are not much accuſtomed to this ſour Sauce in England, but it is very pleaſant.

7. *To roaſt a Calf's Liver.*

Chuſe a very fine Calf's Liver, and lard it very thick with ſmall Slices of Bacon, faſten it carefully to the Spit, and cover it up with Papers; lay it at a Diſtance before a very good Fire, and obſerve its doing, for nothing requires more Time to do nicely.

When it is about half done take off the Papers, and bring it a little nearer the Fire, and at laſt of all, juſt to finiſh it, bring it very near; then ſerve it up in a hot Diſh, with ſome rich Veal Gravy.

8. *To roaſt a Leg of Mutton a la Dauphine.*

Take off the Fat and Skin of a Leg of Mutton, and cut away all the Fleſh about the Shank Bone very clean; put it into Water, and parboil it; then take it out, let it cool, and lard it very thick with pretty large Slices of Bacon; this done ſpit it, and wrap it round with ſome Sheets of white Paper; lay it down

Nº. XIV.　　　3 E　　　　　to

to roaft, and let it be firft placed at a good Diftance from the Fire; toward the End it muft be brought nearer, and Care muft be taken that it have a good Colour.

The proper Sauce is Effence of Ham; but it may be ferved up with Gravy, or with one of the Culliffes.

9. *To roaſt a Chine of Mutton the Italian Way.*

Shred fome Parfley very fine, cut fome Chives fmall, and mix thefe with fome white Pepper beaten; when thefe are well mixed cut fome thin fine Slices of the Lean of a Gammon of Bacon, ftrew thefe all over on both Sides with the Seafoning juft named, and lay them in Readinefs; lay ready alfo fome fine thin Slices of fat Bacon without any Seafoning.

Thefe being prepared take a large fine Chine of Mutton, raife up the firft Skin of it, and draw it off all the Way, only juft at the End, lay the feafoned Slices of Gammon of Bacon upon the Mutton, and over them lay the Slices of fat Bacon plain; when both are on draw the Skin carefully over, and bind it fecurely on with Packthread, then cover the whole with Paper, roaft it, and let it be done carefully; when it is near enough take off the Papers, have fome Crumbs of Bread ready, and drudge it carefully with them; then brown it up, and fend it to Table with good Gravy.

The French put a Raggoo under this and the like Difhes, and thofe who chufe it may follow their Practice, which we fet down for that Purpofe, having directed the making feveral Raggoos in their proper Places, any of which will do for this Purpofe; but the French in this carry their Improvements to Extremes. An Englifh Palate will often be pleafed with their Made Difhes of the plainer Kind, but when they are thrown thus one into another, there is a Confufion of Taftes which takes away all Relifh; befide, when thefe Roafts and Raggoos are kept feparate they make a Variety, but in this new Way of putting one to another, all their Difhes are alike.

This

This I have obferved for the two laft Years here at Bath is growing very common, and the Quality begin to find it out. Mr. Le Strange doubtlefs was a very good Cook, but I heard one who underftands delicate Eating, no Body better, fay at one of the Entertainments of his drefling, that all the Difhes were alike.

C H A P. II.

Of Boiling.

IN the preceding Numbers of this Work we have given the Art of Cookery in its Rudiments, and under thefe common Articles of roafting and boiling have inftrufted the Cook to do the plaineft Things in the plaineft Way : Having thus laid the Foundation for her underftanding perfeftly her Bufinefs, we fhall in this, as in the preceding Chapter of roafting, give her Direftions for the drefling fuch boiled Difhes as are more elegant, yet not expenfive.

The moft moderate Table may, under a proper Management, have great Variety ; there needs not be a Repetition of the fame Joints plainly one after another, unlefs it be the Fault of the Provider or the Cook; for there are many very pretty Things that may be drefled as cheap as plain Joints.

A R T. I. *To boil young Artichokes.*

We have obferved in the Bill of Fare for the fucceeding Month, that Artichokes will be coming in ; they are a Rarity at this Time, and they will appear at Table to more Advantage from a proper Manner of fending them up.

Cut half a dozen of thefe young Artichokes clean from the Stalks, boil them in a good deal of Water with a Nip of Salt in it.

When enough take them out, take out the Chokes, and fend them up with a Sauce of Butter, a little Salt, fome grated Nutmeg, and a very little Vinegar.

3 E 2   2. *Young*

2. *Young Artichokes with white Sauce.*

Boil the Artichokes juft as before, when they are enough tofs up the Bottoms with Butter and Parfley, which muft be feafoned with Sait and white Pepper; put them hot into a Difh, and fend up a Sauce with them made of the Yolks of four Eggs, a quarter of a Pint of rich Veal Gravy, and a Tea Spoonful of Vinegar.

Artichokes may be dreffed this Way at any Bignefs, but 'tis beft when they are thus young.

3. *To boil a Rump of Beef relifhed.*

Shred a very large Handful of fweet Herbs, mix with them fome common Salt and Pepper, and a fmall Quantity of Salt Petre; rub the Beef very thoroughly with this, and let it lie four Days, and no longer.

Then put it into a Pot with a large Quantity of Water, and put in with it four Onions cut in Quarters, and a Bunch of fplit Carrots; add four Bay Leaves, a large Bundle of fweet Herbs, a Handful of Parfley, five or fix Cloves, fome whole Pepper, and a little Salt; boil it well, and as any Scum rifes take it off.

When it is taken out lay it on a Difh, put none of the Herbs or Roots about it, but only ftrew fome frefh Parfley about the Sides of the Difh.

This is a very elegant Way of dreffing Beef; the Salt Petre penetrates beyond what the common Salt alone can do, and the Roots and Herbs give a Flavour to the whole Subftance of the Meat, without altering its Colour in the leaft. It is very agreeable to have this mixed Tafte in eating every Mouthful, and not know whence it comes.

4. *To boil Carp au Court Bouillon.*

Scale and draw a Brace of Carp, and pull out the Fins.

When

When they are thus cleaned put them into an earthen Pan; set on a Quart of Vinegar with a Nip of Bay Salt in an earthen Pipkin, when it is scalding hot pour it on the Carp, and let them lie till cold.

Then set on some Vinegar in a Pan, enough to boil the Carp, put them in, and boil them gently till they are enough; just before they are done throw in half a Pint of white Wine; the Spirit of the Vinegar will by that Time be evaporated, and the Wine will freshen up the Liquor, and give a Richness to the Taste of the Carp: At the same Time with the Wine put in three Bay Leaves, a Spoonful of white Pepper, an Onion, and four Cloves; let all boil up a little that the Carp may be thoroughly done, and receive their Flavour; then take them out, lay them to drain, and send them up in a Napkin, garnished with Parsley.

The Carp this Way have as rich a Flavour as when stewed in Wine.

Our Cooks seeing the Fish sent up at the French Tables in a Napkin thought it was only plain boiled, and under a Notion of imitating it, sent up their Carp in some Places boiled in plain Water, and without any farther Care in the dressing; their Masters found it was not like the other; but this Way it has all the Relish of a stewed Fish, without the Richness of that Sauce we send up with them stewed, which to some is not agreeable.

This is a great Improvement upon the Article of boiling, and may be carried much farther; the Carp here are improved in their Flavour in the same Manner as the Beef in the former Receipt. This may serve as a Hint upon which an ingenious Cook may enlarge very much to her Reputation, and to the Satisfaction of the Family.

5. *To boil Chickens and Asparagus the French Way.*

Our Method in common Families is to dress the Chickens and the Asparagus separate, and send them up in different Dishes; but in this Method of the French
Cookery

Cookery they eat much finer, look more elegant, and coft very little more Trouble and Expence.

Let the Chickens be forced with good Force-meat and boiled, taking Care they are done very white : Thofe who chufe it may do them plain, but the Force-meat is a very great Addition.

Whichever Way the Chicken is done, the Manner of dreffing the Afparagus is to be the fame : Cut it into Pieces of an Inch long, taking only the foft Part, put it into a Saucepan, and parboil it in Water, toward the End adding a little Bit of Butter rolled in Flour ; then take out the Afparagus and drain it.

Set on a Saucepan with a little Butter and a fmall Quantity of Salt, diffolve it foftly, taking Care it does not get brown ; then throw in the Afparagus with fome minced Parfley, a fmall Bundle of Fennel, and fome Cream ; grate in a little Nutmeg, and ftrew in at laft fome Pepper and Salt ; let all this ftew together till the Afparagus is tender, then lay the Chicken in a Difh, and pour the Afparagus and Sauce over it.

6.   *To boil a Pike with Wine.*

This is a German Difh, and one of the Ingredients will feem very extraordinary to an Englifh Cook, but I can affure them, upon frequent Experience, that it is a Difh always very much praifed.

Chufe a Pike of a moderate Size, gut it, and fplit it into two Pieces flat-wife clofe to the Bone ; fet it over the Fire in a Stewpan of Water, and half boil it ; then take it out, fcale it, and put it again into the Stewpan with a very little Water ; put in now with it fome Mufhrooms, Truffles, and Morels cut very fmall, add a Bunch of fweet Herbs, and let it ftew very gently, clofe covered.

The Fire muft be moderate, or elfe it will break the Fifh.

When

When it is near enough take out the Bundle of Herbs, and put in a Cup full of Capers chopped fmall, three Anchovies fplit and fhred fine, a Piece of Butter rolled in Flour, and a Table Spoonful of grated Cheefe.

When all thefe Ingredients are in, pour in a Pint of white Wine, and cover up the Stewpan; let all ftew together till thefe Ingredients are thoroughly mixed, and the Fifh is enough, then take the Pike carefully out, and ferve it up with the Sauce.

7. *To boil Salmon au Court Bouillon.*

Clean the Salmon perfectly well, then with a fharp Knife and an even Hand fcore the Sides of it pretty deep, that it may thoroughly take the Ingredients.

Spread a Napkin on the Dreffer, lay the fcored Salmon upon it, and duft in fome Pepper, Salt, and grated Nutmeg.

Then mix up fome Cloves, Chives, Lemon Peel, Onions, Parfley, Bafil, and Bay Leaves; all thefe are to be cut very fine, and fome more Pepper and Salt is to be mixed with them; then the Salmon is to be dreffed all over very well with this Seafoning.

Make up a Pound of Butter with a little Flour, put this into the Belly of the Salmon, then clofe the Belly, and wrap the Napkin tight about the Fifh to keep all together, and put it into a Fifh-kettle of a proper Bignefs; pour into the Fifh-kettle an equal Quantity of Water and Vinegar, and fet it over a brifk Fire.

When the Salmon is near enough drain off a good Quantity of the Liquor, and pour in a Quart of white Wine, fet it on a Stove, and keep it fcimmering a little Time till the Difh is warmed and all ready for it; lay a clean warm Napkin in the Difh; unfold the Napkin the Salmon is in, and take it carefully out of that, laying it on the other, and garnifhing it with frefh Parfley in pretty large Pieces.

C H A P.

C H A P. III.

Of Broiling.

WE have given the Directions for the common Articles in this Way in our preceding Months, but the ingenious Cook may vary it farther than others think : There is no Method of dreffing fuperior to it in moft Articles, for the Fire is capable of giving a Relifh this Way that the Food cannot have any other.

A R T. I. *To broil Carp.*

Prepare a ftrong and perfectly clear Fire, and warm thoroughly a large and perfectly clean Gridiron, let the Bars be all hot through, and yet not burning hot upon the Surface; this is the perfect and fine Condition of the Gridiron for nice Ufes; for if it be haftily heated the Bars will be hot enough to fcorch the Things laid on them on their outfide, and yet cold enough within to chill it.

The Bars of a Gridiron always muft keep away fo much of the Heat as their Breadth covers, and therefore they fhould be thoroughly hot when the Thing to be dreffed is laid on them.

This Preparation being made of the Fire and the Gridiron, let the Carp be carefully cleaned, the Fins pulled out, and the Scales perfectly taken off; then rub it over with a Piece of Butter, and ftrew fome Salt upon it; lay it on the Gridiron, and watch it very carefully that it do thoroughly, and not too quick.

While the Carp is broiling, the Sauce muft be prepared thus :

Cut to Pieces four Anchovies, half a Cup full of Capers, and a quarter of a fliced Lemon ; feafon thefe with Pepper, Salt, and Nutmeg, and put them into a Saucepan with fome drawn Butter and a little Vinegar ; fend up the Carp when enough with this Sauce hot.

2. *To broil Eels with Green Sauce.*

Chufe large Eels for this Purpofe, fkin them, clean them, cut them in Pieces, and fcore them all about with a fharp Knife; then have ready fome melted Butter, with favoury Herbs, Pepper, Salt, Parfley, and Nutmeg; fet this in a Bowl, and throw the Pieces of Eel, fcored thoroughly, into it; turn and roll them well about, and when they are covered, and penetrated with the Butter and Ingredients, broil them.

While this is doing make the Sauce in the following Manner:

Pound a good double Handful of Sorrel Leaves in a Marble Mortar with a wooden Peftle, and fqueeze out the Juice into a Bowl.

Cut an Onion into very fmall Pieces, cut fome Capers fmall, and mix up thefe with fome drawn Butter; when thefe are mixed up put in the Sorrel Juice, ftir this well in, then fqueeze in the Juice of a large Seville Orange, and fprinkle in fome Salt and Pepper; when all is mixed thoroughly and heated together, fend it up with the Eel.

3. *To broil an Eel pitchcock'd.*

This the French call the Englifh Way of dreffing an Eel; and, though not of their own Invention, they are fond of it at their beft Tables.

Chufe a large fine Silver Eel, rub it well with Salt, then wipe it thoroughly with a Towel; this takes off the Slime.

Skin it when this is done, and cut it into four Pieces or Lengths, put thefe into a Bowl, and pour upon them half a Pint of white Wine, turn them and roll them well about in the Wine.

After this take the Pieces out of the Wine, and cut Notches on the Back and Sides at fmall Diftances from one another.

When the Eels are thus far prepared, make ready a Stuffing thus:

N°. XIV.   3 F   Crumble

Crumble fome Crumb of white Bread very fmall, fhred fome favoury Herbs, Parfley and Chives very fmall, mix thefe with the Bread, and then grate over it a little Nutmeg, and ftrew on fome Cloves bruifed, and fome Pepper and Salt ; laft of all add the Yolks of three Eggs boiled hard, and a good Piece of Butter.

Fill up the Notches in the Pieces of Eel with this Stuffing, and get as much of it to hang about them as you can, then put them carefully into the Skin, tie it up faft at both Ends, and pick Holes in it with a Needle to prevent its burfting; thus prepared lay it on a Gridiron, and broil it very carefully.

While the Eel is doing make Sauce of fome Anchovies and a few Capers, fome Butter, Pepper, Salt, and a little Vinegar.

The Sauce being ready and the Eel done enough, take it up, draw off the Skin, and ferve it up with this Sauce.

This Method with Sauce is our Way entire; the French, who are very fond of the Eel done like the Sauce, generally fend it up dry, with only a little Juice of Lemon.

4. *To broil Mackarel.*

First mix together in a deep Soup Difh fome fweet Sallad Oil with fome Salt, Pepper, and a good deal of whole Fennel.

This being in Readinefs clean and gut the Mackarel, then cut them in Gafhes upon the Back, and lay them in the Oil and Ingredients, turn them feveral Times about that they may be well feafoned, and then wrap each of them up in a good Bundle of the wet Fennel.

While the Mackarel are thus preparing for the Fire, let that and the Gridiron be made ready for them : This is to be managed exactly as for the broiling of Carp, wherefore it need not be repeated here.

Lay

Lay on the Mackarel rolled in the Fennel, and keep a watchful Eye upon them that they be done equally and thoroughly.

While the Fiſh are broiling make the Sauce; it muſt be done thus:

Mince ſome Capers, ſhred ſome ſavoury Herbs, and pick ſome Gooſberries; the beſt Way is to cut theſe as the Capers, but many chuſe them whole; whichever Way is preferred, theſe with the Herbs and Capers muſt be put into ſome clarified Butter, then grate in ſome Nutmeg, ſome Salt, and a very little Vinegar; when the Fiſh are done lay them carefully in a warm Diſh, and ſerve them up with this Sauce.

C H A P. IV.

Of Frying.

WE ſhall in this Article, as in the preceding, now ſet down ſome very eſſential Points in elegant Cookery.

A R T. I. *To fry Chickens in a Marinate.*

Mix together in a ſmall Bowl a Pint of Vinegar, half a Pint of Juice of Lemons, and ſome Salt and Pepper; ſtir all this together, and put to it ſome Chives cut very ſmall, four Bay Leaves broken, and half a dozen Cloves bruiſed; when all is well mixed ſet it by, covered with a China Plate.

This is called the Marinade, and when any Thing is put into ſuch a Mixture it is ſaid to be marinated.

Chuſe a couple of fine young Chickens, cut them into Quarters, and put them into this Marinade, turn them at Times that they may be well ſoaked in it, and let them lie in the whole three Hours in it.

While the Chicken is ſoaking in the Marinade, make the following Batter: Beat up three Eggs in a little Salt and Water, add to this a quarter of a Pound of melted Butter, and ſome fine Flour, juſt

enough

enough to thicken it for the proper Covering of the Quarters of Chicken.

Set on a Stewpan with a large Quantity of Hog's Lard, take out the Chicken from the Marinade, drain it, then wipe it dry in a clean Napkin, prefling it gently; give the Batter a thorough beating-up, and then dip the Pieces of Chicken in it; fee they be well covered, and then drop them into the Lard in the Stewpan.

Let them be done enough; have a Difh warmed ready for them, and fome fried Parfley; take the Chicken out of the Lard when it is of a fine brown, lay the Pieces handfomely in the Difh, and garnifh them with the fried Parfley.

This is a favourite high Difh among the French.

Sometimes they ufe Pieces of Chicken fried in this Manner for Garnifh in large Difhes, but there is a fhorter Way for that Purpofe.

2.   *Fried Chicken for Garnifh.*

Cut a fmall Chicken into Quarters, dip it in Vinegar, and fet on a Stewpan of Lard.

When the Lard is very hot take the Pieces of Chicken out of the Vinegar, wipe them dry, flour them over very well, and put them into the Lard; they will in this Manner fry to a delicate brown, and do perfectly well for Garnifh as the other.

If any chufe to tafte them they eat prettily, but not like the former.

Some give this eafy Method as the true Way to marinate Chickens, but that is a great Error; the French make a Diftinction between thofe for Shew and thofe which are to make a regular Difh; they fometimes, as has been faid before, ufe the true and perfect marinated Chickens for Garnifh, but this is an Error, at leaft a needlefs Expence and Trouble: It is however a greater Miftake to bring that which was only intended for a Garnifh as the proper Difh for the Table.

3. *To*

3. *To fry Veal marinated.*

Cut fome very fine and moderately thick Veal Cutlets.

Mix in a Bowl a Quart of Vinegar and half a Pint of the fatteft Broth; put in five bruifed Cloves, an Onion cut to Pieces, a whole Leek, a Lemon fliced, four Bay Leaves, and fome chopped Parfley.

Let the Veal Cutlets be put into this Marinade, and turned frequently for two Hours.

Then fet on a Stewpan with a large Quantity of Hog's Lard; when it is very hot take out the Veal, dry it in a Cloth, dip it in a Batter made in the fame Way of that for Chickens defcribed in the firft Article, and fry them in the Lard till they are of a fine brown.

In this, as in the former Articles, fuch as chufe to fave the Trouble and Expence of Batter, may drudge the Cutlets with Flour, and it will anfwer the fame Purpofe; but the other Way makes the more elegant Difh.

4. *To fry Mullets.*

Scale and gut the Mullets, melt a good Quantity of fine Butter, and when it is ready pour it into a Soup Difh; cut Gafhes upon the Backs of the Mullets, and dip them in the Butter; then fet on a Stewpan with a good Quantity of clarified Butter, fry the Mullets in this, and when they are enough lay them on a warm Difh, and make a Sauce for them as follows:

Pour into a fmall Saucepan fome of the Butter out of the Pan, mix with it fome Anchovies and Capers, and fqueeze in a little Orange Juice; grate a little Nutmeg into this, and pour it into the Difh with the Mullets.

Other Fifh may alfo be fried this Way; or when they have been foaked in the melted Butter they may be broiled.

Some

Some have thought this cutting and foaking in Butter to be particular to Fifh that are to be broiled, and that it is not needful to fuch as are for frying; but they do not underftand the Principles of Cookery; the Intent of it is to foak the whole flefhy Part of the Fifh, and there is no other Way of doing it.

If the Fifh be put into the clarified Butter without cutting, the infide Flefh, not being foaked, never is mellow, and if cut without foaking it is very little better, for the Outfide of the Cuts hardens at once in the hot Butter, and nothing can be done to foften it; but in this Way there is a foft Mellownefs that gets into the whole Flefh of the Fifh, and then there being fo much crifp Outfide to it, the whole is very agreeable. There is no Way fo proper for frying moft frefh Water Fifhes.

5. *To fry Oifters.*

Put into a fmall Soup Difh an Onion cut to Pieces, fome Bafil, three Bay Leaves, four bruifed Cloves, fome Pepper and Salt, and a few Leaves of Winter Savoury; fqueeze upon thefe the Juice of half a dozen good Lemons; ftir all well together with a Silver Spoon, and cover it up with another Difh.

When this is done pick two or three Score of fine large Oifters, (Rock Oifters are the beft for this Purpofe) open them, and put them into a Sieve to drain away all their own Liquor.

When this is drained off put them into the Soup Difh to the Lemon Juice and Ingredients, turn them frequently, and let them lie thus two Hours.

While the Oifters are in the Marinade make a Batter of Flour, Salt, and Water, and the White and Yolk of one Egg; when thefe are well mixed pour in half a Tea Cup of melted Butter, ftir all about that they may be perfectly mixed, and if the Batter be of a due Thicknefs all is right; if not, add a little Flour to thicken or a little Water to thin it, as there is Occafion.

Set

Set a Pan over the Fire with fome clarify'd Butter, when it is melted and hot take out the Oifters one by one ; lay them on a Napkin, and fpread another over them to dry them ; when dry'd take them up one by one, dip them in the Batter, and fee they be very well cover'd over with it, and then drop them into the Pan.

Let them be fry'd very brown, and as they are taken up let them be laid carefully upon a clean warm Napkin, fpread over a warm Difh, and fent up without any Sauce, garnifhed with fry'd Parfley.

The moft material thing for doing them perfectly brown, is to keep the Butter very hot in the Pan.

On Faft Days Butter is ufed, on others Lard.

6. *To fry Pike.*

This is to be done with the Affiftance of a flight Marinade; 'tis cheap, eafy, and of great Advantage to the Fifh in every Refpect.

Midling Pike are better than large for frying.

The firft thing is to make the Marinade, which is to be done thus :

Pour into a Difh a Quart of common Vinegar, put to it two Bay Leaves, a Bundle of Sweet Bafil, and a few Leaves of Penny-Royal; add a little grated Nutmeg, two Cloves, and a Tea Spoonful of whole Pepper.

Split the Pike open and cleanfe it perfectly well, then cut the Back in feveral Places with deep Slafhes, lay it in the Marinade and turn it once in half an Hour.

When it has lain two Hours, fet on a Pan with a good Quantity of Hog's Lard. When this is melted and very hot, take out the Pike from the Vinegar, fpread a Napkin under and another over it, make it very dry, and when that is done drudge it very well with Flour; put it into the Pan when the Lard is very hot, and it will fry brown and delicately.

While

While the Pike is frying the Sauce is to be made thus; melt fome Butter and put in a couple of Anchovies without the Bone fhred very fine; add a Spoonful of chopt Capers, and a little White Pepper, and laft of all fqueeze in the Juice of a fine Seville Orange.

Lay the Pike upon a warm Difh, and fend it up very hot with this Sauce.

The French for this Sort of Sauce oil their Butter, but this does not agree fo well with an Englifh Stomach.

When the Sauce is made this Way the Anchovies need not be bon'd, but only fplit and put in, and the Butter ftrain'd off thro' a Sieve.

CHAP. V.

Of Baking.

WE fhall here, as in the preceding Articles, give the ingenious and intelligent Cook Receipts for a great many very pretty Difhes, which probably he never imagined would be had from this fort of Dreffing.

1. *To bake Plaife.*

Mince fome Chives, fhred fome Parfley very fine, and cut fome Savoury Herbs, and Sweet Bafil very fmall; mix thefe together, then grate in fome Nutmeg, ftrew over them fome Pepper and Salt, and fet this in Readinefs.

Rub the Infide of a Baking Difh well over with frefh Butter; then ftrew this Seafoning all over it, that it may ftick in good Quantity to every Part.

Chufe fome large and fine Plaife, clean them perfectly, cut off the Heads and Tails, and lay them regularly and evenly in the Difh. When this is done pour in a Gill of ftrong Lifbon Wine, and ftrew over them a little Pepper, Salt, and grated Nutmeg; and then drop in fome melted Butter in fmall Quantity.

Laft

Laſt of all get a large Quantity of very fine Crumb of Bread, ſtrew this carefully and evenly over them, and let it be thick; ſend them to the Oven, and let them be baked to a fine Brown.

When they come home from the Oven, make ſome Anchovy Sauce; warm a Diſh, take the Plaiſe one by one carefully out of the Pan they were baked in, and lay them handſomely in the Diſh : The Sauce is then to be poured in, and they are to be ſent up hot.

The French put in Champaigne inſtead of Liſbon Wine; and ſome of our Cooks who fancy every thing muſt be good that is dear, are for following that Practice; but we can aſſure them from repeated Experience, that Liſbon is in every reſpect preferable on this and all other Occaſions of Cookery: The Spirit of the Champaigne flies off immediately, and the flavour is very bad.

2. *To bake Rabbets.*

This tho' it have but a plain Name, is an exceedingly elegant Diſh.

Chuſe a brace of very fine Rabbets, ſkin and clean them, ſave the Livers, and cut the Rabbets into Quarters; cut ſome Bacon into thick ſhort Pieces for Larding, and with it lard the Quarters of the Rabbets.

When the Rabbets are thus prepared, fit the Diſh for Larding. Cover the bottom of it with Pieces of Fat Bacon and Veal, a Slice of one and a Slice of the other, and before theſe are laid in, let them be well ſeaſoned with Pepper and Salt, ſweet Herbs and Spices; then as they are laid in the Diſh ſtrew among them ſome Onions, Carrots and Parſnips, cut into ſmall Pieces, and ſome Chives and ſhred Parſley over all.

Make a good Quantity of Seaſoning of the ſame Ingredients, and ſtrew it over the Quarters of the Rabbets: Place them carefully in the Diſh, and then ſtrew more of the ſame Seaſoning over them.

Cover them up and send them to a hot Oven; while the Rabbets are Baking there must be a rich Sauce made for them in this Manner.

Put some Slices of Veal and some Slices of Bacon into a Saucepan, with some Carrots and Parsnips cut to Pieces. When it begins to stick to the Bottom of the Saucepan, drudge it with Flour, pour in some rich Gravy, and cut in some Mushrooms and some small Cloves and Nutmeg; when it has boiled some Time, put in some burnt Crusts of Bread. Then pound the Livers of the Rabbets and mix them with the whole, let it all scimmer some time together, and then strain it off.

Put this into a deep small Stewpan, when the Rabbets come from the Oven, take them carefully out of the Pan; drain them and put them into the Stewpan with this Sauce. Let them scimmer up a little, and then lay them carefully in a Dish, and pour the whole over them, send them hot to Table.

3. *To bake a Pike.*

Chuse a large and fine Pike, scale it, clean it perfectly, and cut out the Bone at the Back, in such a Manner that the Head and Tail may hang on by a Skin.

The Flesh being thus all taken out, clear away the, Bone and mix with the Flesh some Flesh of Eel and Carp; season this with Pepper and Salt, and put it into a Marble Mortar; beat it to a Mash and add a little Nutmeg, some Mushrooms, some shred Parsley and a few Chives.

When all these are together, pour in half a Pound of melted Butter and a large Tea Cup of Bread Crumb and Cream beaten together in a Saucepan; last of all add the Yolks of four Eggs raw; beat all well together, and then put it all into the Skin of the Pike, fill it carefully, sew it up, and the Head and Tail being left on, the whole Fish will seem as natural as if it were entire.

This

This is what the French call forcing of any Thing.
The Pike being made up in this Manner, put into
a Baking Pan fome Slices of Onion, fome fhred
Parfley, fome Chives, and a little Pepper and Salt.
Pour fome melted Butter among thefe, and then
drudge on fome Flour.

Rub the Pike all over with melted Butter, lay it
carefully in the Difh with fome of thefe Ingredients
over it; and put fome Parfley over all.

Then fend it to the Oven, and when it is very
Brown it will be enough: Lay it on a warm Difh and
fend it up.

This is a very elegant Difh, and the French eat it
without any Sauce; they have it fent up to Table in
a Napkin, and the Reafon is very plain, for it has
all the Ingredients of a rich Sauce within it.

Some prefer a fharp Sauce with it; fome chufe.
Gravy, and fome a Butter Sauce. We fhall in the next
Chapter give Directions for making a variety of thefe, of
which the Reader may take his Choice; but certainly
the beft Way is that which the French Practice, who
invented the Difh, that is without any.

C H A P. VI.

Of Sauces.

THIS is a large Article and a great deal of the
Elegance of Cookery depends upon it; we
have told the Cook of the feveral common Sauces,
and many of the more elegant ones already, but there
remain feveral behind which are equally worthy of her
Notice for Elegance and Cheapnefs.

A R T. I. *Anchovy Sauce with Gravy.*

Split three Anchovies, take out the Bones and cut
them very fmall.

Put

Put a quarter of a Pint of very rich Veal Gravy into a fmall Saucepan, and feafon it with Pepper and Salt; put in the Anchovies, and a Tea Spoonful of Vinegar, let it all fcimmer together and then fend it up.

This is the Anchovy Sauce that Foreigners eat with Roaft Meat: They fometimes make it richer, ufing Cullis inftead of Gravy.

2. *Truffle Sauce.*

Peel half a Dozen Truffles, wafh them perfectly clean in Spring Water, and then wipe them dry; cut them very fmall, and put them into a Saucepan with fome rich Veal Gravy, or with fome Cullis of Veal and Ham; let it fcimmer fome Time over the Fire feafon it to the Tafte with Pepper and Salt, and fend it up hot.

This is a Sauce the French eat frequently with Butchers Meat.

They make Sauces of Mufhrooms and of Morells in the fame Manner, and they are very fine: In this refpect they proceed upon much better Principles than we in our Cookery; our Sauces have generally Butter for their Foundation, but it is a bad Ingredient.

3. *Mufhroom Sauce for boiled Fowls.*

Put into a Saucepan half a Pint of Cream and a quarter of a Pound of Butter, ftir them one way till the Butter is melted and the whole is thick, then put in half a dozen frefh Mufhrooms cleaned and cut, or in their Place a Spoonful and an half of pickled Mufh-rooms, and in either Cafe a good Spoonful of Mufh-room Liquor. This is the Sauce; and the proper garnifh for the Difh is fliced Lemon.

4. *Brown Celeri Sauce.*

Chufe a large bunch of fine Celeri, pick it, wafh it very clean, and cut it into very fine thin Slices, boil it gently in a fmall quantity of Water till it is per-fectly tender, then add fome Pepper and Salt, and

a Couple

a Couple of Blades of Mace, and grate in a little
Nutmeg; this done let all fcimmer again together,
and then add a Piece of Butter rolled in Flour, and a
Glafs of red Port Wine; boil thefe a little, then put
in a Spoonful of good Catchup, and half a Pint of
rich Gravy.

This is a Sauce much more of the Nature of the
French Cookery than the former, and it is very much
fuperior to it: The other is fimple, but pleafant; this
is very fine and high flavoured.

5. *Liver Sauce.*

Bruife the Liver of a boiled Fowl, with a fmall
Quantity of the Liquor of the Fowl, till it is perfectly
broke and diffolved; fet on a Saucepan with fome
frefh Butter, melt it carefully: Shred fome Lemon
Peel very fine, and mix it with the Liver and the Liquor; when the Butter is perfectly melted put this in,
and mix it thoroughly together.

When it is all hot fend it up, and garnifh the Difh
with Lemon.

This is a plain Englifh Sauce, and is very much
inferior to thofe which we have given from the French
Cookery; but it is proper for us to give the practical
Cook Directions for all Sorts, that fhe may be able
to give Satisfaction in all Families; and this is a
certain Rule, the more Things fhe knows the better
fhe will do every one of them.

6. *Poverade.*

Poverade is a Sauce very much ufed among Fo--
reigners; whoever has looked into any of their Books
of Cookery will remember that they order many of
their Difhes to be fent up with Poverade, though few
of them have taught the Way to make it, which is
this:

Put into a Saucepan half a Pint of Vinegar, and
four Table Spoonfuls of Veal Gravy, add to this three
good Slices of a Lemon, an Onion cut to Pieces, and
a whole

a whole Leek ; feafon it with Salt, and add a good deal of whole Pepper.

Set this on the Fire to boil gently for fome Time, and when it is enough ftrain it through a Sieve into a Sauce Boat, and fend it up hot.

'Tis a very odd Sauce to thofe who are not ufed to it, but it is relifhing, and when the Palate is familiarized to it none pleafes more.

We fee a Number of thefe among the French, and one great Recommendation of them is, that they do not fpoil the Tafte of the Meat, which we drown and overwhelm with our feveral thick Sauces with Butter.

We have obferved that a great many of the nice Difhes of the French are fent up dry, or without any Sauce, the Ingredients of Sauces being within themfelves.

Many fend up Poverade with thefe, and it is a very good Method; it at the fame Time gives a Relifh, and does not in the leaft take off from the Tafte of the Difh itfelf, which is a great Concern.

C H A P. VII.

Of Culliffes.

WE have already fhewn what Culliffes are, and what is their Ufe and Purpofes; they need not be very numerous, but it may be proper to add two or three to what we have given already refpecting this Article.

A R T. I. *Cullis of white Meat.*

Boil four Eggs, take out the Yolks, and grind them in a Marble Mortar; roaft a fine large Fowl, and when it is enough take off the Skin, bone it, and take off all the white Flefh.

Blanch a quarter of a Pound of fweet Almonds, and beat them well in a Mortar with the Yolks of

the

the Eggs, then put in the white Meat from the Fowl, and again beat all together.

Cut fome Slices from a Gammon of Bacon, and fome thin Cutlets of Veal, cover the Bottom of a Stewpan with thefe, and cut in fome Onion, Carrot, and Parfnip in thin Slices ; put in no Liquor, cover this clofe up, and fet it over a very gentle Fire in a Stove.

When it begins to ftick to the Bottom pour in fome fine rich Broth.

A great deal of Care is to be taken to watch the Time of putting in the Broth, for if it be poured in too foon the Cullis will not have its true Flavour, and if it be let alone till the Meat ftick too much to the Pan it will not be of a proper Colour.

When it has had one ftew up with the Broth put in fome Truffles wafhed and cut into very thin Slices, fome Morels, half a dozen Mufhrooms, a Leek, a couple of Onions, and four Cloves, and laftly a Hand-ful of fweet Bafil, then put in about two Ounces of Crumb of Bread, and let it all fcimmer till it is enough ; this will be known by the Condition of the Veal.

When that is enough take it out, and then put in the pounded Mixture from the Mortar ; this will dif-folve in the Liquor with a little ftirring, and when it is well diffolved let the whole fcimmer a quarter of an Hour over a gentle fteady Fire : It muft not boil up, for that would change the Colour. This is the great Concern, and if the whole be conducted accord-ing to thefe Obfervations and Directions it will be perfectly rich, and yet not at all brown. This is the Condition in which it is perfect and fit for Ufe.

Pour all into a Sieve with a large Soup Difh underneath, and work the rich Part of the Cullis well through ; the Veal would keep a great deal of the fine Part hanging about it if it were left in, therefore this Method of taking that out before the other put into the Pan is founded on Reafon.

This

This is to be fet by to be in Readinefs for enriching of Soups, and for Sauces, and all other elegant Occafions where the Difhes are of white Meat. It will keep fome Time good.

2. *Cullis of Partridge.*

This is a very high-founding Difh, but there is no great Expence attending it; a Brace of Partridges will make a good Quantity of it.

The Method of doing it is exactly the fame as in the former Receipt, wherefore it needs not be repeated here, and all the Difference is the ufing Partridge inftead of Fowl.

For this Purpofe the Partridges muft be roafted but little, and then fkinned; the Bones muft be taken out and thrown into the Stewpan with the Veal and Bacon, and the Flefh taken from the Breaft and other Parts muft be beat up with the Yolks of Eggs and Almonds; this is then to be mixed with the Liquor when the Veal and the Partridge Bones are taken out, and the whole is to be finifhed up and ftrained off in the fame Manner.

The Flavour a Brace of Partridges thus ufed gives to a good Quantity of the Cullis is hardly to be credited; one would fuppofe it made of nothing but Partridges, and it is very rich.

3. *Cullis of Mufhrooms.*

This is a Cullis of very great Ufe, and one of the richeft and higheft flavoured of all; it is made a different Way from all the others, and with lefs Trouble.

Chufe a good Quantity of large well-grown Mufhrooms, fkin them, and clean them well; fet on a Stewpan, and put into it half a dozen good Slices of Bacon, the fatteft you have; when this is heated pour in the Mufhrooms, brown them together over a Stove till they begin to ftick to the Bottom.

Then

Then ſtir them about again, duſt in a little Flour, and brown them well with that.

When this is done put in ſome rich Broth of Veal or Beef, let it boil up about two Minutes, but not more, and then ſtrain it off into a Pan.

Put into this ſome Cruſts of Bread, let them ſtand till thoroughly ſoaked, and then heat the whole together; when hot pour it through a Sieve, and the Liquor will run thick into a Bowl or Diſh ſet underneath, and will make an excellent Cullis.

This will keep, and will be ready to give any Diſh a very high Flavour.

C H A P. VIII.

Of Broths and Soups.

UNDER this Head we ſhall give ſome of the plainer and ſome of the more elegant and rich Kind.

A R T. I. *Breakfaſt Broth.*

This is a Broth the Foreigners make in great Quantities together, and it keeps very well ſeveral Days; thoſe who breakfaſt upon it think it improves in the ſtanding. It is made thus:

Take the Chine Part of a Rump of Beef, a Neck of Veal, a couple of Scraggs of Mutton, and two Fowls, ſet all theſe over the Fire in a very large Pot of Water, and keep them ſcimmering all Day.

When the Chickens are pretty well boiled take them out, cut off the white Meat from their Breaſts, tear the Bones aſunder, and put them in again; the white that is cut from the Breaſts put into a Marble Mortar, and at the ſame Time throw a large Piece of Crumb of Bread into the Pot.

Pound the Chicken in the Mortar, and when the Bread is ſoaked put in ſome of it, and work it well with the Chicken.

N°. XV.   3 H   Strain

Strain off the Broth through a Sieve into a large Stewpan, while it is hot ftir in the pounded Chicken and Bread, fet it over the Fire again, and feafon it to the Palate; then fet it by for Ufe.

2. *Broth for French Soups.*

The laft-defcribed Broth was intended for eating as it is, this is only to ferve for Soups, and almoft any of them may be made of it: The Culliffes are added, and make Soups according to their Names and Natures, and in the fame Manner other Ingredients.

The Soups are named from thefe, but the Foundation may be the fame in all, and nothing does better than the Broth now to be defcribed.

Lay down a large Leg of Mutton to roaft, when it is pretty well done take it up, take off the Skin, and put it into a fmall Copper with a good Quantity of Water; put in alfo a good Quantity of coarfe Beef cut to Pieces, and fome Veal cut alfo to Pieces.

The Water muft be cold when the Meat is put in, and the Fire under it muft be gentle.

Let it boil foftly, and as any Scum rifes let it be gently taken off.

When it has boiled fome Time add a couple of large Fowls, and throw in at the fame Time a good Quantity of Onions, Carrots, and favoury Herbs, feafon it with Pepper and Salt, and when it is very ftrong ftrain it off, and fet it by for Ufe.

The Service of a Quantity of this Broth is continual, and for many Purpofes ; a large Family fhould never be without it, and it is worth while to keep it in many fmall ones, for with a careful marketing and proper Choice of the Ingredients, it comes very cheap, and it will be at all Times ufeful, any little Addition making a good Soup from it.

3. *Soup Sante the Englifh Way.*

We have given in a former Number the Method of making Soup Sante according to the French Practice ;

this,

this, which Foreigners call the Englifh Way, makes a Variety, and is a very fine Soup.

Make fome Broth and Gravy in the fame Manner as is done for the French Soup Sante, and for the Receipt turn back to the Defcription of that in the former Part of this Work.

Inftead of the Herbs ufed in the French, put into this a good Quantity of Carrots and Turnips; they muft be cut into long flender Pieces as big as a Quill, and an Inch long; give the Turnips two or three boils in Water to blanch them, and blanch the Carrots by a longer boiling; when they are thus prepared ftrain off the Water, and put them into two Quarts of the Gravy, add the Cruft of two French Rolls, and boil thefe well together till the Roots are perfectly tender.

To fend this up to Table have a Knuckle of Veal boiled, place this in the Middle of the Difh, and pour the Soup to it; garnifh it with Pieces of Carrot and Pieces of Turnip boiled tender.

4. *Pea Soup called Puree.*

Chufe fome fine green Peafe, put them on the Fire in a fmall Quantity of Water, give them one boil or two, and then pour away the Water, ftrain the Peafe in a Sieve, and put them into a Marble Mortar; beat them to a Mafh, and fet them by in a Difh in Readinefs.

Set on in a Saucepan half a Pound of Butter and a quarter of a Pound of Bacon cut in Dice; add two Onions cut fmall, a Sprig of Thyme, a little Parfley, fome Pepper, Salt, and four Cloves bruifed, and add to thefe the Cruft of two French Rolls; fet the Pan on a moderate Fire, and ftir it all carefully about till the Bread is crifp and the whole well done.

Pour in three Quarts of rich Broth; let all this boil up well, and from Time to Time fkim off the Fat; when it is all clean from Fat put in the pounded Peafe, ftir it well together, and let it boil up well, then ftrain

the

the whole through a Hair Sieve, and it will come through very thick and fine; put some soaked Bread into the Dish, and if it be to go up plain pour in the Soup without any Thing more.

This is a common Way in some Families, but the Inventors of this Dish always put something substantial in the Middle.

A Knuckle of Veal boiled separate, and taken up just at the same Time with the Soup, is a very good Thing to put in the Middle, and in other Places they frequently put Pigeons; or at this Time of the Year a Green Goose or a Duckling is an elegant Addition.

The right Garnishing is split Cucumbers, with the Core taken out and boiled.

5. *Blue Pease Soup.*

This is the Soup for Winter as the other is for Spring, and as the Season is scarce yet advanced far enough for the green Pease, we shall give the Receipt with the others.

Set on a Quantity of blue Pease in a good deal of Water, let them boil till they are perfectly tender, then strain off the Water, and beat up the Pease to a Mash in a Marble Mortar, as the others in the former Receipt.

For all the other Particulars, they are to be done in the same Manner as in the green Pease Soup; and for colouring of it there must be put in some Juice of Spinach along with the pounded Pease, or the Juice of the Leaves of green Wheat; this last is a Secret known to few, and it has the finest Effect of all; the Colour from Wheat Leaves is finer than from any Thing, and it has not the least ill Taste.

6. *Asparagus Soup.*

This is a Soup made of Asparagus in the same Manner as the other is with Pease, and there is no other Difference, except that in this Soup the Asparagus is not to be pounded, but cut in small Bits,

pro-

properly boiled, and put in when the Soup is ready to fend up.

Some make entire Peafe Soop, and put in the Afparagus; others ufe no Peafe, but only put the Afparagus into the Cullis; the firft Way makes the Thicker and Richer, but the latter the more elegant Soop. The Tafte of the Afparagus is very much loft in the Peafe Soop, but when the Peafe are omitted, it is very high.

C H A P. IX.

Made Difhes.

WE have in the preceding Numbers given many of thefe, but there are innumerable others.

A R T. I. *Artichoaks with Cream.*

Boil fome Artichoaks in Water till they are enough. Then take them up, tofs up the Bottoms with Butter in a Stewpan; and put in fome Cream and with it a few Chives and a Bunch of Parfley; when it is enough thicken the Sauce with the Yolks of Eggs, add to it a little grated Nutmeg and fome Salt, and ferve it up hot.

2. *Fillet of Veal with Collops.*

Cut what Collops you want from a Fillet of Veal, then fill the Udder with rich Force Meat, tie it round and Roaft it; lay the Udder in the middle of the Difh, and the Collops which muft be done by the fame time round it, and fend it up with Gravy and Butter, garnifhing the Rim of the Difh with Lemon.

3. *Ragoo of Hogs Feet and Ears.*

This is a very pretty Difh, and is to be made of the Souced Feet and Ears in this Manner.

Take as many of each as is convenient out of the Pickle they were fouced in, and cut the Ears into

long

long thin Slices, put them into the Stewpan with a
Glafs of white Wine, half a Pint of Gravy, a Piece
of Butter rolled in Flour, and a good Quantity of
Muftard; cut the Feet in two, and put in alfo. Stir
all together till it is of a good Thicknefs and well
done, then fend it up in a Soop Difh hot.

4. *A Fricaffee of Pigeons.*

Kill eight fine young Pigeons, cut them into fmall
Pieces, and put them into a Stewpan with a Pint and
Half of Water, and a Bundle of Sweet Herbs.

Let them ftew gently for fome time, then add a
Pint of white Wine, fome Pepper and Salt, three
Blades of Mace, half a Dozen whole Cloves, an
Onion, and a good Piece of Butter rolled flightly in
Flour.

Cover all up and let it ftand over the Fire ftewing,
till there is no more left than juft enough for Sauce.

Then beat up the Yolks of three Eggs, and grate
in a little Nutmeg. Take out the Onion, and the
Sweet Herbs; thruft the Meat all up to one fide of
the Pan, and let the Gravy run to the other; mix in
the Egg with this, and ftir it carefully elfe it will run
to Curds. It will thicken the Sauce up very finely.
When this is done, mix all together, and put in a
Spoonful of Vinegar.

Set it on once again covered, to heat throughly together, and while it is doing for the laft Time, fry
fome Oifters, and toaft fome thin flices of Bacon;
when all is ready, pour the whole out of the Stewpan into a Difh, fprinkle the Oifters over it, and lay
the Bacon round, then garnifh the Difh with flices of
Lemon.

5. *Afparagus with Cream.*

Cut the Green and tender Part of Afparagus into
Pieces of an Inch long, fet it on for a few Minutes
in boiling Water to blanch it; then pour it into a
Cullander; let it drain; fet on a Stewpan with fome
Butter,

Butter, tofs up the Afparagus in it, and take Care it do not get too Fatty.

Seafon the Afparagus a little with Pepper and Salt, and put in a good Quantity of Cream.

While this is doing over a gentle Fire, beat up the Yolks of a couple of Eggs in fome Cream, with a little Sugar ; pour this in and ftir it well about that the Eggs mix evenly and well with the reft, and then ferve it up.

This is a very elegant and agreeable Way of eating Afparagus, and fuits the Nature of Englifh Cookery, wherefore it pleafes at an Englifh Table generally better than the Way next to be defcribed, which being done with Gravy is higher and richer, and fuits more the Tafte of Foreigners.

6. *Afparagus with Gravy.*

Cut fome fine young Afparagus into Pieces of an Inch long, rejecting all the bad Part.

Blanch thefe by boiling them a few Minutes in Water, then ftrain them off and tofs them up in a Stewpan with Hogs Lard ; throw into the Stewpan with them fome Chervil cut fmall, a little Parfley alfo cut fmall, and a Leek whole.

Pour in a little rich Broth, take out the Leek, and feafon the whole with Pepper and Salt, and a little Nutmeg.

Let thefe fcimmer together till the Afparagus is per-fectly well done, then take off all the Fat, and pour in fome rich Mutton Gravy ; laft of all fqueeze an Orange over the whole, and ferve it up hot : It eats more rich than Afparagus any other Way.

7. *Afparagus boiled plain.*

We boil Afparagus whole and fend it up with But-ter, and with a Toaft under it : The French do not fend it to Table fo plain as this, and their boiled Afparagus which they call plain, is very much pre-ferable to ours. It is done thus :

Boil

Boil the Afparagus when perfectly cleaned, in fome Water with a little Salt, and take Care it be not over done.

Set the Afparagus a draining, and in the mean Time make the Sauce; this muft be made of Butter, Pepper, and Salt, fome Vinegar and the Yolks of a couple of Eggs beat up; thefe laft are to be carefully mixt in, and kept from Curdling, and they will thicken it very finely : This done, the Afparagus is to be laid in a Difh evenly and regularly, and the Sauce is to be poured over them without any Toaft under the Afparagus.

8.   *Beef a la Vinaegrotte.*

Cut a large fine fteak of Beef, beat it very well that it may be thoroughly Tender, and fet it on in a Stew-pan covered up with fome Water feafoned with Salt and Pepper.

When it has ftewed fome Time, open the Pan, and pour in a Gill of white Wine.

Put in at the fame Time half a dozen Cloves, a Bay Leaf, and a Bundle of favoury Herbs.

Set it on a gentle Fire covered, and let it ftew till the Liquor is almoft all confumed.

Then pour the whole together into an earthen Pot, and let it ftand till cold ; when cold fend it up garnifhed with Lemon, and fharpened with a very little Vinegar.

This is an uncommon kind of Difh in England, but it is very convenient, cheap, and agreeable ; we are fond of having fomething cold in fmall Families, and the Cook who would render herfelf moft agreeable in fuch, fhould make it her Bufinefs to get out of the common Tract, and know how to make fuch Difhes as will add to the Variety of the Table, without adding to the Expence. Few Things are Cheaper than this, and I never faw it brought to a Table tolerably done, where every body are not pleafed with it. In my fmall way I have ferv'd it often, and have been
asked

afked for more Receipts for the making it, than for any one Difh that I remember. I made it in a manner Univerfal at Bath, in the Year 1749. M. B.

9. *A Bifque of Pigeons.*

This is a great and very elegant Difh, fit for the greateft Table, and very grand at a middling one, on any particular Entertainment.

Some fine Broth, and fome ftrong Gravy, muft be prepared for this Difh; the Cook has had general Directions for this, but on the Occafion of this Bifque, it is beft to refer her to the Directions we have given for making Soop de Sante the French Way. Let the fame Broth, and the fame Gravy, be made for this as for that.

Put together a good Quantity of this, and fet it over the Fire, put in the Crufts of two French Rolls, and let it boil together fome time; then pour in a Quart of rich Veal Gravy, boil all up together, and when the Bread is very foft, pour the whole into a Sieve, with a large Pan underneath; rub the Bread about the Sieve with a Spoon, and moft of it will go through.

Boil eight Squab Pigeons very tender; boil alfo a Pound of Coxcombs tender, firft Blanching them in Water; thefe and the Pigeons muft be boiled in good Broth, and the Coxcombs muft be done half an Hour longer than the Pigeons, that they may be perfectly Tender.

While this is doing, cut a fine blanched Sweetbread into fmall fquare Pieces like Dice; cut alfo a few of the fmalleft of the Coxcombs, and fry thefe together in fome Butter, till they are of a fine Brown.

Garnifh a large Soop Difh with a rim of Pafte, and lay fome of the largeft and fineft of the Coxcombs round it; then pour in the Bread and Gravy, lay in the Pigeons and the Coxcombs regularly, and laft of all put in the Sweetbreads and Coxcombs fried Brown. Send it up hot. It is an expenfive Difh, but is efteemed one of the moft elegant.

10.   *Boucons.*

This is another very rich Diſh, it is of French Contrivance, and has its Name from that Language, which ſignifies a Mouthful ; it is made thus : Cut ſome very fine Veal from the prime Part of the Fillet, into longiſh thin Slices ; lay theſe upon a Dreſſer.

Cut out ſome Bacon in thickiſh Pieces as if for Larding, but ſomewhat larger, and cut ſome of the lean Part of a Raw Ham in the ſame way ; lay theſe one of Ham and one of Bacon all the way along the ſlices of Veal, then ſeaſon all with Pepper and Salt ; grate over ſome Nutmeg, and ſtrew Chives and Parſley both cut ſmall, and ſome Savoury Herbs.

When all is ſeaſoned, roll up the ſlices of Veal handſomely, and tye them round with Thread.

Set on a Stewpan with ſome ſlices of Bacon at the Bottom, over theſe lay ſome thin ſlices of Beef, then ſeaſon it very well, and lay in the Boucons of Veal ; over theſe lay a layer of thin ſlices of Beef, and over them ſome more Bacon, then cover up the Stewpan cloſe, fixing down the Edges of the Cover with Paſte ; let the Fire be very gentle under it, and lay upon it ſome lighted Coals of Charcoal.

The Seaſoning for the Stewpan is to be the ſame with that already deſcribed for the Boucons ; ſo nothing more is needful than to make enough of that.

When the Stewpan has thus been kept hot Top and Bottom for half an Hour, the Boucons will be enough.

The Coals are then to be thrown off ; the Cover is to be removed, and the Layer of Beef and Bacon taken off.

Then the Boucons are to be taken carefully out, the Threads that tie them are to be cut and unwound, and they are to be placed in a Diſh ſlanting, to let the Fat drain thoroughly from them : They will be thus done very Tender and Delicate, and will

have

have the Relifh and Richnefs of the Beef, as well as their own Tafte and Seafoning. They are to be fent up hot in a Soop Difh, with fome very rich Gravy.

This is at prefent the general method of eating Boucons; but fome make them a yet richer and more expenfive Difh, by fending them up in the moft coftly Ragoos. This is not only adding a great deal of Trouble and Expence, but making the Difh much lefs delicate; this adding one rich Thing to another, takes away the Tafte of every Difh, and when Cookery is carried to fuch a height, it has not the Effect of Judgment at all. A Scullion could put all the rich Ingredients at random together, and they would have the fame Effect as in fuch Jumbles of Mixture: The Skill of the Cook is to be employed to know how to feparate the Ingredients, and which to join one to another for the Difh.

11. *Blanched Cauliflowers in Gravy.*

Fill a large Boiler half full of Water, put into it a fmall Quantity of Flour, a Piece of Butter, two or three flices of Fat Bacon and fome Salt.

While this is heating, prepare the Cauliflowers by picking and wafhing them very clean.

When the Liquor boils, throw in the Cauliflowers, and let them boil fo long till they are about half done; then take them out, and fet them in a Cullander to drain.

The Cauliflowers are now what the French call Blanched. This is the Practice of Blanching, with what they call Fat Water; fometimes they only fcald Things in plain Water, and call that Blanching of them, but this is the beft Method; and always to do them nicely, it fhould be in this Water, which they call the Fat Water. When the Cauliflowers are drained dry, put them into a deep Stewpan, they are not to be thrown in at Random, but laid regularly; and then pour upon them fome rich Veal Gravy, or the Cullis of Veal and Ham, defcribed in a former

Number. Let there be as much of the Gravy or Cullis as will juft cover the Cauliflower, and fet the whole over a gentle heat in a Stove.

When it is ftewed enough, roll about an Ounce of Butter in a good deal of Flour, mix in the Flour by pinching it together with the Fingers, and then break the Butter into five or fix Pieces; put thefe in at different Parts of the Stewpan near the Edge, and keep it moving over the Fire till the Butter is melted, then put in a drop or two of Vinegar, and take it up. The Cauliflowers are thus full impregnated with the Tafte and richnefs of the Gravy.

12.   *To ftew Chardoons.*

Chardoons are the Stalk of a kind of Artichoke blanched in the fame Manner as Celeri, but they are larger, and are as white as Cream on the infide : When they are rightly managed, and properly dreffed, they are a very great Delicacy.

They are to be firft Blanched, but in a particular Manner. Set on a good deal of Water in a Pot, put to it fome Salt, three or four Slices of fat Bacon, a quarter of a Pound of Beef Suet, and half a Lemon with the Peel, fliced thin.

While this is heating, pick the Chardoons, and cut them into fhort Pieces, when it boils throw them in, and let them boil in it till they begin to be tender, then drain them.

Set on a Stewpan with fome good Gravy; put in a bundle of Sweet Herbs, fome Marrow of Beef, and a fmall Quantity of grated Cheefe. Stir all thefe about, and then put in the Chardoons, which will by that Time be very well drained from the blanching Water.

Keep them Stewing in this, till they are perfectly Tender; then fkim off all the Fat, and heat a Salamander, or for want of that a Firefhovel, red hot in the Fire. Hold this over the Chardoons in the Stewpan, and turn them at Times that they may be perfectly

fectly Brown all over; then ferve then up with the Gravy.

13. *Boiled Chickens with Onions.*

Boil young fine Chickens in the ufual Way, only taking care they be done with great Nicety; as they doing, make the Sauce in this Manner.

Brown fome Butter, and put in a couple of Onions minced fmall, a Spoonful of Capers chopped, and two Anchovies picked and boned and fhred very fmall; tofs thefe up together, and then add fome rich Veal Gravy.

Lay the Chickens in the Difh, and pour this Sauce carefully over them. Thefe are proper for a firft Courfe.

CHAP. X.

Of Puddings.

THIS is a Store almoft as inexhauftible as that of made Difhes, and as they ferve on many Occafions, when other Foods cannot be eat, it is the Bufinefs of an accomplifh'd Cook to be Miftrefs of many Sorts.

ART. I. *Blood Puddings.*

Set on in a large Saucepan a Quart of Grots, or what they call whole Oatmeal, that is the Oats prepared for grinding into Meal, with as much Milk as there is of them. Boil this well, and fet it by all Night; this will make the Grots Swell, and be very tender.

Next Day fhred a Pound and Half of Beef Suet, and feafon it well with Pepper and Salt.

Cut very fine a Handful of Penny-Royal, a Handful of Thyme, and a Handful of Parfley, put thefe into Pan, with the Grots and Milk, and add to them three Pints of Blood.

Hogs Blood is commonly ufed for this Purpofe, but Sheeps Blood will do as well; there will be no Difference

in

in the Tafte of the Puddings. Stir this well together, then put in a Pint of Cream, ftir all again, and laft of all put in the Suet.

When all is perfectly well mixed, fill it into clean Guts, or boil it in a Bag.

The boiling a Blood Pudding in a Bag is lefs common, but it is an excellent Difh. In the other Cafe they are to be filled into the Guts juft as we have directed for the Marrow Puddings, and then tied up in proper Lengths.

Thefe make what we call Black Puddings, a coarfe Difh in the common Way, becaufe they are made in a flovenly Manner ; but when thefe Directions are followed they are worthy to appear at any Table.

Before they are fent up they muft be boiled, and then broiled or fried; and the handfomeft Way of ferving them is, to fend up a fmall Difh with thefe and White Puddings together.

2. *Puddings of Fowls Livers.*

Thefe are another Kind of the Puddings that are to be ferved up in Guts boiled and broiled : They are not very common in England, but they are very good, made at a fmall Expence, and fhew Variety in an Article where few know how to introduce it.

Black Puddings, and White or Marrow Puddings, are all we generally make of this Kind in England, but it will bear much more Change.

Get Fowls Livers to the Quantity of a Pound Weight, mince them very fmall, and add to them a Quarter of a Pound of Hog's Fat minced alfo very fmall, and a Pound of the Flefh of a fine Fowl or Capon carefully picked from the Bones; the white and red Meat minced together.

Pound a little Cinnamon, and four or five Cloves, add to this fome Pepper and Salt, a little grated Nutmeg, and fome favoury Herbs cut very fmall ; mix all thefe together for a Seafoning, and with this feafon the mixed Meat.

When

When all this is well mixed together, beat up the Yolks of fix Eggs in fome fine Cream in a large Bowl; by Degrees get in a Quart and half a Pint of Cream in all, and then bring in the reft of the Ingredients, mixing all very thoroughly together.

Fill fome Guts with thefe in the Way we have directed for filling of Marrow Puddings, and then tie them in proper Lengths.

Boil them, and afterwards broil them, when they are to be fent up to Table.

Thefe Puddings may be boiled in Water in the common Way, but it is an Addition to them to boil them in Milk with a little Salt; and the beft Way of fending them to Table is with Black Puddings and Marrow Puddings all in a Difh together, laid one by one; their Colour fhews the Difference.

5. *A Calves Foot Pudding.*

Pick the pure flefhy Part from fome Calves Feet, leaving out the Fat and the Brown; get a Pound of this fine white Meat, and mince it very fmall; pick all the Films and Skins from a Pound and half of Suet, mince that alfo very fine, and mix it well with the Foot.

Break fix Eggs, beat up all the Yolks and three of the Whites; grate the Crumb of a Roll, and wafh and pick a Pound of Currants.

All thefe Things being ready put in fome Milk to the Eggs, with a little Salt and a Duft of Sugar; grate in fome Nutmeg, and add a Handful of Flour.

When all thefe are beat and mixed very well, put in the reft of the Ingredients; being mixed to a proper Confiftence put it in a Bag, and boil it a long Time; it fhould be put on early in the Morning to be ready for Dinner.

For Sauce pour fome plain melted Butter over it, and mix fome melted Butter, white Wine, and Sugar in a Sauce-boat.

4. *A Yorkshire Pudding.*

This Pudding is to be made when there is a good Piece of Beef roasting.

Beat up four Eggs, mix them with a Quart of Milk, a little Salt, and as much Flour as will make it into a middling stiff Batter ; a little stiffer than is fit for Pancakes.

Set on a Stewpan with some Dripping, when it boils pour in the Batter, and let it bake on the Fire till it is near enough.

Then turn a Plate Bottom upwards in the Middle of the Dripping-pan under the Meat, and set the Stewpan with the Pudding in it on the Plate ; the Fat from the roast Meat will drop upon it, and the Fire coming freely to the Top of the Pudding, will make it of a fine brown.

Let it stand thus till the Meat is done, then drain off the Fat, and set the Stewpan on the Fire again to dry it perfectly well.

When this is done put it into a Dish, cut a Hole in the Middle of it that will hold a China Cup, fill this with Butter melted plain, and so send it up to Table.

This is an errant English Dish, but it is a very good one.

5. *A Sweet-meat Pudding.*

Cover a Dish with fine Puff Paste Crust, and lay it in nicely and thin ; slice very thin an Ounce of candied Orange Peel, the same of Lemon, and the same of Citron Peel ; lay these carefully all over the Bottom of the Dish.

Beat up eight Yolks of Eggs and two Whites, and mix with these half a Pound of the finest Loaf Sugar powdered and sifted, and the same Quantity of Butter carefully melted ; beat all these well together, and pour them into the Dish over the Sweet-meats ; send it directly to the Oven.

The

The Oven ought to be but moderately hot when this is put in, and three Quarters of an Hour, or a little more, will bake it.

C H A P. XI.

Of Pies.

OF thefe there yet remain feveral very nice and elegant Kinds to be added to what we have defcribed in our former Numbers.

A R T. I. *A Devonſhire Squab Pie.*

Cover a Diſh with good Cruſt.

Slice fome fine Apples, and cover the Bottom of the Diſh with them, firſt ſtrewing in a little Sugar, and when they are in ſtrew a little more over them.

Cut a Loin of Mutton into Steaks, feaſon them very well with Pepper and Salt, and lay a Layer of them evenly over the Apples; over this lay another Layer of ſliced Apples, with a very little Sugar ſtrewed over it, and over thefe a Layer of ſliced Onions.

Over thefe lay another Layer of Mutton Chops, then another of Apples and Onions; then pour in a Pint of Water, and clofe the Pie; fend it to a Baker's Oven, and let it be well done.

This is a particular Diſh, fome are very fond of it; a right Devonſhireman will prefer it to the beſt and niceſt of all that follow.

2. *An Oiſter Pie.*

Blanch three Pints of Oiſters, and take off the Beards.

Mince one fine Anchovy, and as much Parſley as will make a Table Spoonful; mix this with the Anchovy, and with two Spoonfuls of grated Bread, and a Quarter of a Pound of Butter; add by Way of Seafoning a little Pepper, and about a third Part of a

Nutmeg, not grated, but fhaved thin with a Pen-knife.

Thefe Things being mixed and fet in Readinefs, make the Pafte thus :

Mix together fix Ounces of Butter and a good Handful of Flour, with two Table Spoonfuls of cold Water.

Part the Pafte into two Pieces, and roll them out.

Cover a Patty-pan with one of the two Pieces of rolled Pafte, then divide the Mixture of Anchovy and Parfley into two equal Parts, fpread one half regularly over the Bottom of the Patty-pan on the Cruft, and upon this lay the Oifters. The Patty-pan ought to be of fuch a Size that the Oifters may lie about three deep.

When they are in put the Remainder of the Parfley upon them, and lay on it a couple of thin Slices of Lemon ; then fprinkle a little beaten Pepper over the whole, and pour in very gently at different Places about three Table Spoonfuls of the Oifter Liquor.

Then cover it with the other Piece of Cruft, and turn up the Edge of the Pafte an Inch high ; fend it to be baked three quarters of an Hour before you want it ; then cut up the Cover, fqueeze in a Lemon, and cutting the Lid carefully into about fix Pieces, lay it over the Pie.

Some bake this Pie without any Lid, but it is beft thus.

3. *A Patty of Calf's Brains.*

Take out the Brains from a Calf's Head, clean them carefully, and fcald them ; fet them by.

Cut off the Tops of a hundred of Afparagus, and blanch them in hot Water with a little Butter and Flour ; let the Afparagus ftand to be cold ; then roll up fome Force-meat in little Balls, and boil half a dozen Eggs hard, take out the Yolks, and lay thefe, the Brains, the Afparagus, and the Force-meat into

the

the Patty together; fend it to the Oven, and when it comes home fqueeze in the Juice of half a Lemon, and add fome drawn Butter and fome Gravy.

This makes a very elegant little Difh to ferve up hot.

4. *A Pheafant Pie.*

Pick and draw a Pheafant, lard it with large and thick Pieces of Bacon, and lay it by till a Stuffing is made for it in this Manner:

Cut fome Parfley very fine, mince a couple of Truffles and fome frefh Mufhrooms, rafp fome Bacon, and fhred a few Chives; mix all thefe well together for the Stuffing, and ftuff the Body of the Pheafant carefully with it.

Raife the Cruft for a Pie of a proper Size, cover the Bottom with fcraped Bacon, and ftrew over this fome Pepper and Salt, a couple of Blades of Mace bruifed, three whole Cloves, and fome fweet Herbs chopped very fine; lay in the Pheafant, and ftrew a good deal of the fame Seafoning over it; then lay upon it fome Slices of Veal cut very thin, fcrape fome Bacon over this, and add fome fmall Pieces of Butter; over all this lay fome broad thin Slices of fat Bacon, and then put on the Lid, and fend it to the Oven to be well baked.

While the Pie is at the Oven peel and flice half a dozen Truffles, put them into a fmall Saucepan with half a Pint of rich Gravy, or as much Cullis of Veal and Ham before defcribed.

Keep thefe hot till the Pie comes from the Oven, then raife up the Lid of the Pie, and take off the Veal and the Bacon that covered the Pheafant, take off the Fat, and pour in the Gravy and Truffles.

It is a moft elegant Difh.

5. *A German Lamb Pie.*

Cut a Quarter of Lamb into fmall Steaks and Pieces, and lard them all very well with fmall Pieces of Bacon.

3 K 2   Make

Make a Seafoning for them thus :

Scrape fome Bacon, cut two Bay Leaves, grate in half a Nutmeg, bruife three Cloves, and fhred fome Chives and a good Quantity of favoury Herbs; mix all thefe very well together, and take fo much of each of the principal Ingredients that the whole may amount to a good handfome Quantity.

Cover the Bottom and Sides of a Difh with good Cruft, fpread a Quantity of this Seafon over the Cruft, and then lay in the Pieces of Lamb, placing them regularly and handfomely ; then fprinkle among them and over them the reft of the Seafoning, and pour in fome good Broth.

Cover up the Pie, and fend it to a Baker's Oven, with Orders to let it ftand three Hours.

When it is about coming home prepare a Raggoo of Oifters, as we have directed, and taking off the Lid of the Pie, firft fkim off the Fat that fwims upon the Gravy, and then pour in the Raggoo of Oifters hot.

6. *Carp Pie.*

Chufe a Brace of fine Carp, and have a large Silver Eel in Readinefs, fcale and gut the Carp, cut the Flefh of the Eel into long flender Slips of the Shape of Pieces of Bacon ufed for larding, and with thefe lard the Back and Sides of the Carp very thick.

This is a nice Piece of Cookery, but with a fteady Hand and due Care it may be done very prettily, and is a vaft Improvement to the Fifh.

Let the Cook remember we have ordered a Silver Eel for this Purpofe, and let her take Care to chufe fuch a one, and the fineft fhe can get. The yellow Eels are apt to tafte muddy, and any Flavour of this Kind deftroys the Tafte of the Carp. The Whitenefs of the Belly is not the only Mark of an Eel that is perfectly fine ; the right Colour of the Back is a coppery Hue, very bright ; the Olive-coloured are inferior, and thofe that are more tending to the green are worfe.

The

The Carp being thus larded, mix together fome Pepper and Salt, fhave in a little Nutmeg, and add two bruifed Cloves, and one Bay Leaf chopp'd fmall; with this Seafoning fprinkle the Fifh well over on both Sides, and ftick in different Places on it feveral fmall Pieces of Butter.

The Carps thus prepared are ready for baking; let a Cruft be raifed for a Pie, and the Shape of it be fuch as conveniently to hold the two Carp; or a very pretty Pie may be made with one large Fifh. Strew fome of the Seafoning at the Bottom of the Pie; put in the Carps carefully, and add a little Fifh Broth, or if there be none in Readinefs, a very little Water. Put on the Lid, and put it into the Oven.

It is moft convenient to bake this Pie in the Houfe, becaufe it muft be taken out when about half done.

At this Time raife the Lid, and pour in a Glafs of Mountain Wine: Clofe down the Lid again, and fet it into the Oven to be done enough.

While the Pie is baking this fecond Time, put on fome Oifters for a Ragoo as we have directed; let it be made by that Time the Pie is done, and raifing up the Lid, pour it hot in, and fend up the Pie hot. It is a proper Difh for a firft Courfe, and will be a Grace to the beft Table.

7. *A Veal Pie.*

Make a good Quantity of Seafoning of Pepper and Salt, Sweet Herbs, grated Nutmeg, and a Blade of Mace; fet this in Readinefs.

Cut a fmall Fillet of Veal into three Parts; lard thefe very well, and cover it thick with the Seafoning: Raife Cruft for a large Pie, fhape it, and fpread over the Bottom a good Coat of Force-Meat.

Lay the three Pieces of larded Veal over this, and between, and upon the Pieces of Veal, lay a couple of Sweetbreads cut into Pieces, and fome Mufhrooms cut fmall.

You

You may add Truffles, Morels, and Artichoke Bottoms, but the Pie will be perfectly good without thefe.

Pound fome Bacon and feafon it with Pepper and Salt, Savoury Herbs and Spices; lay fome of this over the Veal and Sweetbreads, and if at Hand, put in the Crevices between the Meat, a few blanched Afparagus Tops.

Send it to the Oven, and let it be baked two Hours; then cut open the Cruft, take off the Fat, and pour in fome Veal Gravy.

The French pour in Cullis of Veal and Ham. This with the Morels and Truffles makes it look the more elegant; but the Pie is a very fine one without them, and perhaps to a judicious Palate eats better.

8. *Eel Pie.*

Chufe fome fine large Silver Eels, fkin them, clean them, and cut them into Pieces of a Finger's Length.

Pick off the Flefh from the Bones of a Couple of the largeft of them, and make this into a Kind of Force-meat, with the following Ingredients. Cut fmall fome Chives, chop fome Parfley very fine, fhred fome frefh Mufhrooms; and upon all thefe well mix'd together, fprinkle a good deal of Pepper and Salt: Mix the Flefh pick'd from the Bones of the Eels with this, ftir all well together and fet it by.

Raife a good Cruft, and make the Pie of a moderate Height : Cover the Bottom with this Force-meat, and then feafon the Pieces of Eel for the Pie, with the fame Ingredients as were mixed up for the Force-meat.

Lay them carefully and evenly in, and put in fome Sweet Herbs; and over the whole a good deal of Butter.

This done, put on the Lid of the Pie; rub it over with fome Egg, and put it into the Oven.

Have fome very ftrong Fifh Gravy ready, and when the Pie is brought from the Oven, open it;

fkim

ſkim off the Fat, pour in the Gravy very hot, and covering it again ; ſend it up to Table.

This is an Eel Pie for a genteel Table, and is to be made without any great Expence.

Thoſe who have a Mind to make it richer, may eaſily do that : They are only to mix in a good Quantity of Milts of Fiſh, of any of the freſh Water Kind in the Gravy ; and adding Truffles and Morels in good Quantity, to make it a Kind of Ragoo ; and pour this in inſtead of plain Fiſh Broth, or Fiſh Gravy.

We chuſe to give the Cook her Choice in all theſe Caſes, to make a good Diſh plainer or richer : But on this, as on many of the preceding Occaſions, we are to tell her that the Pie will eat better in the Manner firſt directed, tho' it will have a richer Look in the other.

C H A P. XII.

Of Side and ſmall Diſhes.

THESE in general may be ranked among the Made Diſhes, but as they are of a particular Uſe at the Table, we have thought it proper to keep them under a ſeparate Head, that the Cook may ſee them together.

A R T. I. *Tench Patties.*

Pick off all the Fleſh from the Bones of a large Tench.

Half ſtew ſome freſh Muſhrooms, let them cool, and then mince them very ſmall. Pound together in a Mortar a couple of Cloves, a ſmall Piece of Cinnamon, a little cut Parſley, and a few Chives firſt chopped ſmall ; ſeaſon all this with ſome Pepper and Salt, and when well mixed, bring in the Fleſh of the Tench, and a large Piece of Butter, and beat all together to mix it.

Set

Set this by on a Plate, and make fome very rich Puff-Pafte : Make fmall Patties of this, and put into each a pretty large Lump of this Mixture ; clofe them up, and fend them to be carefully baked.

2. *Oifter Patties.*

Pick out half a Dozen fine rich Oifters, and chufe a fine large Silver Eel. Pick the Flefh of the Eel from the Bones, and beat it up in a Marble Mortar, with fome Pepper and Salt, a couple of Cloves, and as much Mountain Wine as will make it foft.

When this is well mixed, lay it by on a Plate, and make fix Patties of fine Puff-pafte.

When the Patties are all laid ready, open the fix Oifters, and taking out one Oifter for each Pattie, wrap it up in a Piece of the Force-meat, and add a Piece of Butter.

Clofe the Patties, and fend them to be carefully baked.

They make a very pretty fmall Side Difh ; or they may be ufed by Way of Garnifh for fome very magnificent Difh of Fifh.

This is the plain and cheap Way of making Oifter Patties. They may be much richer, by the Addition of other Ingredients, as we fhall fhew in the next Article.

3. *Oifter Patties with Carp.*

Chufe half Dozen large and fine Oifters as before, and chufe alfo a fine Carp ; take Care that it be a Male Fifh, and full of Milt. Chufe alfo a large Tench, and a fine Silver Eel.

Pick the Flefh from the Bones of all thefe Fifhes, and beat it up together in a Mortar, with favoury Herbs, Pepper and Salt, Mace and fome white Wine. Then add the Milts of the Fifh, and mix all well together.

This being prepared, make the Patties of the fineft and richeft Puff-pafte Cruft, and into each of them

put

put one Oifter, with a good Quantity of this Force-meat round it ; add a Piece of Butter, clofe up the Patty, and fend it to be baked.

4. *A forced Pigeon.*

Make fome Forcemeat of Veal, as we have directed in a former Chapter.

Chufe a fine young, but fully grown Tame Pigeon, pick and clean it, and ftuff the Breaft with a good Quantity of the Forcemeat, fending the Remainder to be baked.

Boil the Pigeon, and fee that it be done to a Nicety: Then lay it in a Difh, garnifh the Difh with fome of the baked Forcemeat, and pour over the Pigeon fome very thick drawn Butter.

5. *Eggs with Orange.*

Squeeze into a China Bafon thro' a Sieve, a couple of fine well flavoured Seville Oranges; and fee that nothing but the pure clean Juice goes in.

Beat up fix Eggs with a little Salt. Then by de-grees get in the Orange Juice, and mix the whole per-fectly well together.

Set on a Saucepan over a gentle Fire, with fome Gravy, and a Piece of Butter; when it is warm, and the Butter melted, pour in the Egg and Orange, and fet it again over a moderate Fire.

Stir the whole continually, that the Eggs may not burn to the Bottom, and when they are thoroughly done, ferve them up as they come out of the Sauce-pan. The Difh muft be hot they are put into, and they need no Sauce.

6. *Eggs and Sorrell.*

Bruife a large Handful of Sorrell Leaves, and prefs out the Juice; beat up three Eggs, and put in firft a little Pepper, Salt, and Nutmeg, and then the Juice of the Sorrell : When all this is well mixed, melt fome Butter, and pour in this; ftir it about a

little,

little, that it may mix well, and be thoroughly hot. When this is ready, poach the Eggs.

See they be fine and new laid; break them into a China Cup, and flip them into a large Saucepan of very clean boiling Water.

When half a dozen are nicely Poached, lay them regularly upon a Difh warmed for that purpofe, and pour the Sauce over them.

7. *Eggs in Gravy.*

Set on a Saucepan with Water for Poaching fome Eggs, and lay half a dozen fine new laid ones on a Difh ready.

Set on another Saucepan with a Pint of Veal Gravy, a whole Leek, fome Salt and Pepper, and a Blade of Mace whole. Let this fcimmer away while the Eggs are preparing.

When the Water boils for the Eggs, throw in a little Salt, and a quarter of a Pint of Vinegar.

Break the Eggs one by one into a China Cup, and flip them into the boiling Water.

Set a Difh to warm, and as they are poached, lay them in the Difh; one in the Middle, and the others round it.

When they are all in, take off the Gravy, hold a Sieve over the Difh of Eggs, and pour in the Gravy; by this Means it will be clean, and will fall regularly over the Eggs; fend them up garnifhed with hard Eggs quartered.

8. *A Bacon Amlet.*

Cut fome thin Slices of the lean Part of a fine boiled Ham, mince them very fmall, and fet them by.

Cut fome Parfley fine, and mix it up with fome Pepper and Salt: Break eight Eggs and beat them up well; put in the Parfley, and Pepper and Salt, and then a Couple of Spoonfuls of Cream, and half the minced Ham. Beat all this very well together, and then fry it brown.

Chufe

Chufe a Difh fo big as to hold the Amlet, and not let it touch the Sides: Lay it in this, and lay the remainder of the minced Ham round it.

While this is doing, cut fome flices of Gammon of Bacon; beat them well, and then tofs them up with fome melted Bacon, Flour, and good Gravy: When all this has ftewed together fome Time, put in half a Spoonful of Vinegar, and ftrain it off; pour this into the Difh with the Amlet, and fend it up hot.

9. *A Ragoo of Ham, with Sweet Sauce.*

Set on a quarter of a Pint of good Port Wine, a Spoonful of Water, and a ftick of Cinnanon; let it boil up once or twice, then take out the Cinnamon, put in a Spoonful of the fineft Sugar powdered, and half a Tea Spoonful of white Pepper beaten: And when thefe have boiled up once, add a Table Spoonful of grated Macaroon. This is the Sauce.

Cut fome very broad and thin Slices of raw Ham, tofs them up in a Saucepan till they are thoroughly done, then lay them handfomely in a fmall Difh, and pour the Sweet Sauce over them; juft as they are going up, fqueeze in half a Seville Orange.

10. *Lambs Trotters Forced.*

Set in readinefs fome Veal Forcemeat.

Boil two Pair of Lambs Trotters, and when they are pretty well done, take them up, fplit them lengthwife, and take out the Bone.

Fill them up with the Forcemeat, and beat up three Eggs.

Dip the Trotters in the Eggs, and then fry them brown. Garnifh them with fried Parfley, and if any Sauce be fent up with them, it muft be Veal Gravy, but they will do without.

11. *Marrow Fritters.*

Chufe fome fine found Apples that are not too fharp in the Tafte, pare them, take out the Core, and mince them very fine.

Mince

Mince a good Quantity of Beef Marrow, twice as much as there is of the Apple, and put to thefe mixed together, fome fine powdered Sugar.

Set on a Pan with fome clarified Butter; wrap up thefe Ingredients in Puff-pafte, and fry them brown : Strew fome powdered Sugar over them, and let the Difh be hot. Send them up without any other Addition.

12. *A Pearch Ragoo'd.*

Chufe a moderately large and fine Pearch, gut it, and lay it on a Gridiron ; when it is half broiled take it up, and with a careful Hand take off the Skin.

Set on a Saucepan with half a Pint of Fifh Broth, put in an Onion ftuck with Cloves, a Bay Leaf, fome Sweet Herbs, and fome fhred Parfley ; and feafon it with Pepper and Salt.

Let thefe boil up a little, then pour in half a Pint of white Wine ; fet on a fmall Stewpan, and put into it about two Ounces of Butter rolled in Flour : When it is getting brown, pour it into the Saucepan to the Wine and Gravy ; pour the whole after it has had a boil into a very fmall Stewpan ; lay in the Pearch, and let it fcimmer very gently till the Fifh is done enough, then take it from the Fire. Take out the Pearch carefully, fo as not to break it, lay it on a fmall Difh, and ftrain the Gravy over it through a Sieve.

This is a Difh of no great Expence, but it is a very Elegant one. A Brace of Pearch may be done with the fame Trouble as a fingle one, but we are here fpeaking of the fmalleft Difhes.

The French who generally outdo the Matter on thefe Occafions, put a Raggoo of the Fifh kind into the Difh with their Pearch; thofe who chufe to imitate them fo Exactly may find Receipts for thefe Raggoos in the proper Parts of this Work, but the Way here defcribed is preferable greatly.

The Pearch is a Fifh of a particular fine Tafte in it felf, and its Flavour is improved by the Wine and

other

other Ingredients here directed; but when we come to add whole Raggoos of different Ingredients to this, the proper Tafte of the Fifh is loft, and it might as well be any other. This is a general and univerfal Obfervation.

13. *A Ragoo of Coxcombs.*

Pick and clean half a Pound of Coxcombs, put them into a fmall Saucepan, put to them a Bunch of Sweet Herbs, fome Mufhrooms cut fine, and fome melted Bacon; feafon this with Salt and Pepper, and tofs it up over a gentle Heat.

Then pour in a little Gravy of any kind, and covering it up, fet it over a gentle Fire to fcimmer and ftew flowly.

When the Coxcombs are Tender, take out the Bunch of Sweet Herbs, and take off the Fat; and pour it into a fmall Difh, garnifhed with fmall Pieces of fliced Lemon. The French make this Ragoo more expenfive by the Addition of Truffles, and more troublefome by the mixing fome Cullis of Veal and Ham with it: In great Families where thefe Things are in Readinefs, there is no Reafon why they fhould not be ufed, but the Ragoo is a very good, and a very genteel Difh without them.

14. *Livers Ragoo'd.*

Take four or five Livers of large fat Capons, or other large and well fed Fowls; thefe are what the Cooks call fat Livers; feparate the Gall carefully, and throw them into a Saucepan of boiling Water to blanch them.

Throw them out of this into a Bafon of cold Spring Water.

Set on a fmall Saucepan with fome melted Bacon, throw in a few Button-Mufhrooms, a Bundle of Sweet Herbs, fome Salt and Pepper, and laftly the Livers; tofs them up in this, then pour in a little good Gravy, and fet the Saucepan to fcimmer over a gentle Fire.

When

When the Livers are done, take them out, lay them in a Difh, and ftrain off the Gravy; pour this over them, and fend them to Table garnifhed with Seville Orange in Slices.

S E C T.   II.

Of CONFECTIONARY.

ALTHO' we are not yet arrived at the Seafon when the Fruits come in for the Service of the Confectionary, yet there are fome farther Articles under the Head of Creams, and the like, which are to be added here.

A R T. I.   *Italian Cream.*

Put into a Silver Saucepan a Quart of Milk, add to it a little Salt and a ftick of Cinnamon, and fome powdered Sugar ; boil it up two or three Times, that the Sugar may be thoroughly melted, and the Milk get the Tafte of the Cinnamon.

Break five new laid Eggs, feparate the Whites, and mix the Yolks very carefully with the Milk ; ftrain this three or four Times thro' a Sieve into a Difh, place the Difh the laft Time in a Baking Cover very fteady, and put the whole into it, then put Fire over and under it, and continue the Heat till the Cream is of a right Thicknefs ; then ferve it up.

2.   *Cream Toafts.*

This is the Difh which the French call Pain Perdu ; Loft Bread.

Chufe a Couple of nice and well baked French Rolls ; cut them thro' in Slices as thick as ones little Finger, Cruft and Crumb together.

Lay

Lay thefe in a clean Difh, and pour upon them a Pint and Half of Cream.

Mix together fome of the fineft Sugar powdered, and fome Powder of Cinnamon : Duft a little of this over the Slices of Bread ; when they have lain a little Time turn them : Duft on fome more of the Spice and Sugar, and proceed thus till they are very well foaked.

When they are thus tender, get a Slice under them, and take them carefully out without breaking.

Break half a Dozen Eggs, rub the Bread all over with the Egg, and then fry it in clarified Butter.

There is no great Difficulty in this Difh, but there is required a great deal of Care; otherwife the Sops will be broke or burnt, which would fpoil all. They muft be fried to a good Brown, and kept whole.

Drain the Butter very well from them, and place them in a fmall Difh, putting Sugar round them ; and ferve them up hot.

3. *Goofeberry Cream.*

We are juft getting into the Seafon when the Ufe of Fruit is coming in, and fhall here begin with the earlieft.

Put a Quart of Goofeberries into a Saucepan, with juft as much Water as will cover them, fcald them, and then with a Spoon force the foft Part thro' a Sieve.

To a Pint of this Pulp beat up three Eggs.

While the Pulp is hot, put in a Piece of Butter as big as a Wallnut, and as much Sugar as will fweeten it agreeably ; when this is done, put in the Eggs, and mix them carefully with the Pulp, ftir the whole again over a gentle Fire for a few Minutes, and then fet it by to cool ; juft as it gets cold, put in a Spoonful of Spinage Juice, or green Wheat Juice, and a Spoon-ful of Orange-Flower-Water; then fend it up.

S E C T.

S E C T. III.

Of Pickling and Preserving.

A R T. I. To Pickle Artichoke Suckers.

THE Artichoke juft at this Seafon produces thofe young Fruit which are fit for Pickling, and the Houfekeeper is not to mifs the firft Opportunity of doing it, for none that can be got in the fucceeding Part of the Year, will be fo perfectly tender.

The Artichokes muft be cut for this Ufe while fmall, and before the Leaves grow hard ; and they muft be pickled in this Manner.

Wafh them carefully, and pick away any Thing that may hang about them ; pare off the hard Ends of the Leaves, and lay them in an earthen Pan.

Set on a Saucepan of Water, with a Nip of Salt in it ; when it boils, pour it upon the Artichokes, and cover them up.

Open the Pan at Times to ftir them about; and when they are pretty well fcalded, take them out, and lay them to drain.

Have a large Glafs ready for them, and when they are quite cold and drained, lay them carefully in, putting between and among them fome Pieces of Mace, and fome fhaved Nutmeg.

Fill up the Glafs with diftilled Vinegar, and fet it by.

2. To Pickle Artichoke Bottoms.

Chufe for this Purpofe fome Artichokes which are grown to their Bignefs, but are tender and very fine, fet them on in a Pot of Water, and when they are tollerably well boiled, take them up.

Pull

Pull off all the Leaves foftly and carefully, that the Bottom may be left as entire as poffible: Then take off the Chokes, and obferve that the Knife do not any Way touch the Artichoke Bottom, becaufe it is certain to fpoil the Colour.

While the Artichokes are picking, put into a large earthen Pan fome Spring Water, and a little Salt; as they are picked, put them carefully into this; and when they are all in, let them lay an Hour.

When they are taken out of this Water, let them be laid to drain; and when dry, place them regularly in the Glafs or Jar where they are to be kept; put in among them fome Blades of Mace, fome fhaved Nutmeg; and pour in as much fine Vinegar as will cover them, and half a Hands-breadth more; then pour upon it fome melted Mutton Fat; and when all this is cold, tye over the Glafs or Jar with a wet Bladder firft, and then with Leather.

3. *Englifh Bamboo.*

There is a fine and much efteemed foreign Pickle, which is made of the tender Shoots of the Bamboo Cane, and in England an Imitation if it may be made with young Shoots of Elder. They are as Tender, and by that Time they have been four or five Months Pickled, are very little different in Tafte. They are to be done thus.

Cut fome of the fine young Shoots of Elder, that appear toward the end of May.

Mix up a ftrong Brine of Salt and Water, and fet it by you in a Pan. Cut the Shoots into Lengths, and Peel them carefully; as they are peeled, throw them into the Water, and let them lie there four and twenty Hours.

Then take them out, wipe them with a Napkin, and lay them to be perfectly dry on the outfide.

While they are drying, prepare the Pickle thus. Mix together equal Parts of White Wine and Beer Vinegar; and to two Quarts of this, put two Ounces of white Pepper, two Ounces of Guinea Pepper, and three Ounces of fliced Ginger ; half an Ounce of Mace, and the fame Quantity of All-Spice.

Set all upon the Fire, place the Shoots regularly in a large Jar, and when the Pickle boils, pour it upon them.

Stop the Jar with a Bung, and fet it before the Fire to keep it hot, for two or three Hours, often turning it about, that it may every where heat equally. Then fet them away to cool, and tie the Jar over for keeping.

4. *To Preferve Afparagus.*

Set on a Saucepan with a good Quantity of Butter and fome Salt ; cut off the white Ends of the Afparagus, and when the green Part is cleaned and fcraped, put it into the Butter, let it boil up for three or four Minutes, and then put it into a Pan of cold Spring Water.

Let them remain in the Water till quite cold, then take them out, and lay them to drain till quite dry.

Place the Afparagus regularly at its length in a Pan, and ftrew in fome Salt, fome Cloves, and Slices of Lemon.

Mix an equal Quantity of Vinegar and Water, and pour upon them : Then lay a Piece of Linnen Cloth two or three Times doubled over them, and pour upon this fome melted Butter.

This will preferve them without letting in the Air, fo that they will keep their Colour. They will keep the Year round, and may be at any Time dreffed, as if frefh gathered : They will alfo look very well at their Length among a Variety of Pickles.

5. *To Preferve Artichokes Moift.*

Boil up a large Quantity of Water with fome Salt, and fet it by that the Foulnefs of the Salt may fettle to the Bottom ; and then pour off the clear Brine into a large earthen Pan.

Set

Set on another Pot of Water without any Salt; when this boils, put the Artichokes you intend to preferve into it, and let them boil till they are fo far foftened, that the Choaks may be got out.

This done, wafh them in two or three Waters, and when they are perfectly clean, put them into the Pan of Brine; cover them in the Brine, and pour on it a good Quantity of melted Fat, fo that the whole Surface may be covered a Finger's-breadth Thick.

Then tie over the Pan with a large wet Bladder, and cover that with a Piece of Leather. Set it in a Place where it may ftand quiet, and lay a Board upon it, to prevent any ones fhaking it, which might break the Fat, and let in the Air, and the Brine then could not preferve them.

Artichokes will keep thus all the Year round, and when they are to be ufed, they muft be taken out fome Time before, and fteeped in frefh Water; this and the boiling will take out the Saltnefs of the Brine, and they will eat nearly as well as when frefh.

Some put Vinegar to the Brine that is made for them, but it is of no Ufe in the preferving of them, and it is liable to this Difadvantage, that they get a Relifh from it, which the boiling does not take away.

6. *To preferve Artichokes dry.*

Set on a large Pot of Water, and when it boils throw in the Artichokes; let them lie fo long that the Choaks can be taken out, and then take them up.

When the Choaks are out, let them be laid to drain; and when they are perfectly dry, let them be put into a moderate Oven, and kept there till they be as dry as Wood: Then keep them in a dry Place, and they will remain good throughout the Year. The Way to ufe them is this; two Days before they are to be eaten, put them into a large Veffel, and pour upon them fome warm Water; let the Veffel ftand in a warm Place, and let the Artichokes lie in it two

3 M 2   Days,

Days; in that Time they will grow foft and tender, and will appear perfectly frefh.

They are then to be boiled in the common Way; only lefs Time will do them, becaufe of the foaking.

They eat very well, but not like fuch as are frefh gathered.

The Ufe of thefe Things is to give Variety at Seafons when they are not to be had otherwife, and at thefe Times they always furprize the Company; and this is one of the Points at which a complete Cook aims.

SECT. IV.

Of Brewing and Liquors.

CHAP. I.

Of Wines.

WE have given Directions for the making of fome of thofe Wines which, from their being produced by an artificial Method here, are called *Made Wines*; and we fhall deliver the Receipts for many more in the Courfe of this Work; but at prefent we fhall endeavour to fet that Matter of Made Wines in a better Light to the Houfekeeper and Houfewife than they generally ftand, and fhew her how fhe fhall preferve her Wines from the Faults fo common in thofe made by the Generality of People, and recover the Credit of the Made Wines of England.

The Made Wines of this Country lie under fome Difcredit at prefent, and this, which is owing only to the Miftakes of thofe that make them, is commonly charged upon the Nature of the Thing itfelf.

I have

I have tafted many of thefe Wines in different Families here at Bath, and round the Country, and moft of them very unpalatable; but then I have been able to fhew Wines of my own making that had not any of thefe ill Flavours, as many are ready to teftify.

In the fame Manner I have heard of the Unwholfomenefs of Made Wines; but I never found it in my own, nor have any of thofe complained that drank them, and we have fome here who have drank very freely of them.

I have been told of Headachs and Gripings in the Bowels, and many other Complaints in particular attending upon the drinking of them; but I have ufed myfelf, and many of my Friends, to my own Wines, and we find no Sort of Difadvantage from them.

What I fhall endeavour therefore in the fucceeding Part of the Work under this Head is, freely and candidly to lay before the Publick the feveral Methods I have ufed, and the particular Cautions I have obferved on the different Heads; that every Family who pleafes to be at the fame Pains may have their Wines as pleafant and as wholfome as mine.

Sugar is the Bafis or Foundation of all Wines, from the richeft of the Foreign, to the plaineft of the Englifh Made Wine.

A great deal of Sugar may be procured from the Juice of Grapes; and the Birch Juice, which we make into Wine, may be boiled up to Sugar. In the fame Manner there is a Kind of Maple in the Weft-Indies, the Juice of which in fome Places is made into Sugar, and the Tree is thence called the Sugar Maple; and in other Places the fame Juice is made into Wine. The fweet hardened or candied Subftance we find upon Raifins, which are dried Grapes, is alfo Sugar.

I name this to fhew the Error of thofe who think our Wines cannot be good, becaufe many of them are made of Sugar; we fee by this that Sugar is properly
and

and truly the Foundation of all Wines; and if we examine their Flavours in the fame Manner, we fhall find they are as eafy to be given to our Made Wines, for they are almoft all artificial.

The Art of the Wine Cooper is kept the greateft Secret of any Bufinefs whatfoever; if their Practices were a little more known, we fhould find no Difficulty in giving Body and Flavour to our Made Wines; for moft of what comes out of their Hands is little better.

They know what their Cuftomers expect, and they know how to give the Flavour; that is all.

The Wine Cooper knows People like Port to be deep coloured and rough, and he knows how to give it that Tafte and Colour; for the true genuine Wine of Oporto is not of that Sort: Every one knows genuine Port Wine is quite a different Thing from what is commonly fold under that Name; therefore the Colour and Tafte, and alfo the Brightnefs, and in fome Degree the Richnefs of Port Wine, are owing to Ingredients put in here, and the Art of the Cooper. We may find what thofe Ingredients are, and imitate that Art in putting them together: This is what I fhall endeavour to lay down in the following Sheets, and we fhall then find it no Way difficult to give Body, Flavour, and Colour to our Made Wines; nor will they be unwholfome any more than thofe common at Taverns.

The Wine Cooper makes Sack and Mountain as well as Port, and we may imitate him in thefe as well as the others.

If it be true that thefe People ufe Arfenick and other poifonous Ingredients, thofe we fhall avoid; but in that Cafe it is very plain whofe Wines will be the moft wholfome, thofe at Taverns or ours: If they can only be brought to Perfection by fuch Means, we had rather ours remained imperfect; we had rather they fhould be inferior in Quality than poifonous.

The

The great Art in making Wines in England is to get the Liquor firſt to a proper Conſiſtence, and then to give it a due Fermentation. Thoſe who go about theſe Things are ignorant of the firſt Principles, and that is the Reaſon they miſcarry.

The Houſewife knows how to try the Strength of her Brine by an Egg's ſwimming upon it; ſhe little thinks the ſame Care is neceſſary for the preparing a Liquor for making of Wine: This is a much nicer Thing, and therefore ought to have more Exactneſs; but it is neglected.

I ſhall here lay down a Rule that is univerſal, and will ſerve for many Purpoſes in making of Wine; it is this: That the Liquor be tried the ſame Way. Any Liquor is fit for making a ſtrong Wine that is of the ſugary or grapy Kind, and is rich enough to bear a new-laid Egg; and if not ſo rich it is not fit.

Many of the Juices that are uſed for making Wines are too thin for this, and theſe all miſcarry for that very Reaſon: This ſhould be the firſt Trial, and if they do not bear the Egg, they muſt be boiled away till they will, and then they are fit for working.

C H A P. II.

Of plain Sugar Wine.

TAKE two Hundred and a Half Weight of double-refined Sugar, put this into a Wine Pipe, that is, a Veſſel holding two Hogſheads, and pour in Water till it is within about four Gallons of being full.

The beſt Water is pure Spring Water.

Set this in a Wine Vault, and add four Pounds of freſh Wine Yeaſt, if that be to be had, if not, the ſame Quantity of good Ale Yeaſt will do very well.

Let the Veſſel ſtand undiſturbed, and the Liquor will regularly ferment, and after that will be a Kind

of

of Wine ; it will have a good Body, and will tafte clean, but without any particular Flavour, neither will it have any Colour. This will receive the Flavour of any Fruit whatfoever, by mixing a Part of the Juice of the Fruit with the Sugar among the Water, and a Piece of Turnfole will give it a very good Colour, a fine deep bright Purple, fuch as many admire in Port Wine.

This is a very fhort, plain, and eafy Manner of making any of the Fruit Wines ; and as to the Flower Wines, they may in the fame Way be made by only throwing a large Quantity of the Flowers, fuppofe Clary, Cowflips, or whatever, with the Water : Thus the Sugar Wine, which has naturally no great Tafte of its own, will receive their feveral Flavours ; and being pure and clean, they will be finely tafted in it.

As we have named Turnfole for giving the Colour to the red Wine, it is fit to fhew what the Wine Coopers ufe for the yellowifh ; as Sack, Mountain, and the like ; this is Saffron Paper : A few Sheets of this give the proper Colour to a Hogfhead ; and both Saffron Paper and Turnfole are very innocent Ingredients.

Here therefore is a fhort Account, and a very plain one, of a great Article in the Wine Cooper's Myftery ; and at once a Method of making moft of the common Wines, with lefs Trouble and more Certainty than the Methods ufually known.

We have fhewn in the preceding Numbers, fpeaking of Made Wines, how they are to be kept, and when bottled : To avoid Repetitions, we refer thither for the Particulars, and have given this as a Practice that explains and exemplifies, in a Manner, the whole Matter at once.

The judicious Houfekeeper, who fees how eafily this is to be done, will fmile at long Receipts, and the Detail of Ceremonies laid down in moft Books. We fhall for the Sake of Plainnefs lay down particular

Methods

Methods for particular Fruit Wines, as they come into Seafon in the two or three following Months; but if no other Receipt than this and the following had been given, the good Houfewife of an intelligent Mind, could not have been much to feek for the making any of the numerous Kinds of Englifh Fruit, Flower, or Juice Wines.

A R T. I. *Malaga Raifin Wine.*

We propofe here to lay down the eafy and familiar Way of making this excellent Wine, to which many Things may be added in the fame Manner as to the Sugar Wine, but this is perfect without them.

Chufe fome fine, whole, and fweet Malaga Raifins, put a Quarter of a Hundred of them into a fmall Cafk, and pour upon them feven Gallons of cold Spring Water, cover this flightly, and fet it in a warm Place; let it keep there fome Weeks.

The Water will fwell and burft the Raifins, and the whole will ferment; there will be a hiffing Noife, and a Froth at the Top.

When this is over the Liquor is to be managed as we have before directed, keeping it a proper Time in the Cafk, and then bottling it; and it is a pleafant wholfome Wine, which may be improved in Colour by being tinged to a light yellow with Saffron Paper.

The Time of the Wine's ftanding fhould be about five Months; it is then to be drawn off into another Veffel, and in three Months more it will be fine and fit for bottling; or it may be drawn off in a Decanter as ufed.

The beft Time to put in the Saffron Paper is when it is drawn into the fecond Cafk, and a fmall Quantity is fufficient; this not only gives an agreeable Colour like Mountain, inftead of the watery Whitenefs of the common Raifin Wine, but it helps the fining of the Wine, and gives it a pleafant Flavour.

One Caution muſt be given the Houſekeeper in this Caſe, which is, to take particular Care the Saffron Papers are good and genuine ; they ſhould be bought of the People who cure the Saffron : They have a good Smell when genuine, and a deep Orange red Colour : Too many counterfeit them, and thoſe will give the Wine an ill Taſte.

The right Saffron Papers are what cover the Cakes of Saffron in the drying, but the others are ſtained with Turmerick.

2. *Raiſin Vinegar.*

This comes ſo naturally after the preceding Article, that we could not avoid giving it in this Place ; and it comes alſo ſo cheap that the Houſekeeper ſhould not decline making it when ſhe makes the other.

When the Wine is drawn off in the foregoing Man-ner of making Raiſin Wine, there will remain a Quan-tity of Grounds or Lees, and the Skins and other Fragments of the Raiſins ; for the Quantity of theſe ſet on four Times as much Water, and when it is boiling hot pour it upon them in the Caſk ; cover the Caſk lightly, and ſet it in a warm Place, and there let it ſtand without being diſturbed for ſome Weeks : Nothing more is needful, for the Liquor will in that Time of itſelf become Vinegar, well-bodied, ſound, and ſharp.

Let this be drawn clear off from the Bottoms, and bottled or kept in a Jar or Caſk for Uſe : It ſerves excellently for the larger Pickles.

The ſame Caution is needful to this as to Wine, in drawing it clear from the Lees or Bottoms ; for other-wiſe it will very ſoon decay. If the Settlings be left in any of theſe Wines or Vinegars they will grow muddy and dead, and will never come to any Thing again whatever Care be uſed.

The great Article for preſerving Wines and Vinegars is to get them very clear from the Lees, and to ſtop them cloſe ſo as to keep out the Air, for thoſe are the two Things that bring them to decay.

The

The Veſſel muſt not be ſtopped cloſe while they are fermenting, for then it would burſt; but when that is over, and the Liquor is grown quiet, then the Buſineſs is to preſerve it in the Condition it is in; and this is only to be done by racking it fine and keeping it cloſe from the Air; bottling is the ſecureſt and beſt Method, and in this the proper Care is to ſee them well corked.

When Convenience does not allow of this, they muſt be kept in ſound Caſks, and the Caſks muſt be full.

Theſe are what we have thought proper to deliver in this Place, as the general Rules and univerſal Cautions to be obſerved in the making of Wines, which we ſhall bring into Practice in the Obſervations on the next Month, when the Summer Fruits begin to come in. This will ſerve as the general Method, and they who properly underſtand this, will be able to conduct themſelves in all the reſt with Safety and Diſcretion.

SECT. V.

Of DISTILLING.

CHAP. I.

Of Spirits in general.

A S we have ſhewn in the preceding Section the Method of making Wine and Vinegar from Raiſins, we ſhall begin this with the Way of procuring Brandy from the ſame Materials: This will be a very fine and well-flavoured Spirit, and will anſwer all the Purpoſes of Spirits of every Kind. When made of the common Strength of Brandy, which we

call

call *Proof Spirit*, it ferves for diftilling many Cordial
Waters. When made double that Strength, by recti-
fying it, is what we call Spirit of Wine; and in that
State is fit for making Tinctures, and all other Ufes,
much better than what is bought under that Name :
That, tho' called Spirit of Wine, is really made of
Malt, which gives it a difagreeable Flavour : This is
perfectly fweet, and in every Refpect preferable.

As the Method of diftilling this will lead the careful Houfekeeper to the underftanding the Diftillation
of fpirituous Liquors in general, fuch as the Cordial
Waters, Spirit of Lavender, and the like, we fhall
lay it down particularly here. The Want of a little of
this general Knowledge of the Nature of the Thing is
what fpoils the Family Cordial Waters, in the fame
Manner as the Family Wines are fpoiled for Want of
fome general Informations on that Head; for though
the Apothecaries Cordial Waters excel the Ladies in
Clearnefs and Flavour, it is owing only to their being
more acquainted with the Art of Diftilling; the Ingredients are generally more faithfully and carefully
prepared in the Ladies.

This needful Knowledge of Diftillery we have in
Part inculcated in one of our firft Numbers, and fhall
take this Opportunity of illuftrating what we have
faid there, by Examples in the Diftillation; firft to the
Spirit itfelf, and then with the Addition of fuch
Ingredients as compofe the other favourite Kinds of
Cordial Waters.

C H A P. II.

Of Raifin Brandy.

POUR into a common Still three Gallons of the
Raifin Wine, new made, according to the Direction given in the preceding Section; give a moderate Fire, and there will come over a ftrong fpirituous Liquor.

Tafte

Tafte and try this at Times, and fo long as it is ftrong let it run into the Veffel.

When that is over remove the firft, and place another Veffel under; this will receive the latter Runnings, which fhould be faved fo long as there is any Thing fpirituous in them; this will partly be difcovered by their Tafte, and more certainly by their burning.

A good Way to try this is to throw the Liquor that comes over upon the Still Head hot as it is in the working; fo long as there is any Spirit in it 'twill take Fire, when it does not the fpirituous Part is all come over, and the Fire may be taken out.

The Houfekeeper who has managed carefully will now have two Sorts of Spirit, a ftronger and a weaker.

Thefe may be kept feparate for different Ufes, or diftilled together over again; or the firft may be diftilled alone, and the other kept for feparate Purpofes.

As the Strength of the firft Spirit is uncertain in this Way of fimple Diftillation, the moft ufeful Method of proceeding is to diftil it again to a certain Degree of Strength.

We have Ufes for Spirits, as before obferved, of two Degrees of Strength; the one equal to common Brandy, which is what is called the Proof Spirit, the other of double that Strength, which is what we call Spirit of Wine; this will all burn away when fet on Fire, whereas the Proof Spirit will only burn away in Part, being half of this Strength, and confequently half Water.

The ftrong Spirit made by this Diftillation will be true Spirit of Wine, the others generally fold under that Title having no Right to it.

To bring the Spirit obtained from Raifin Wine to a Proof Strength put it into the Still again, either alone or with the latter Runnings; make a moderate

Fire,

Fire, and obferve what comes off: When it is fomewhat ftronger than Brandy in the whole, and the Runnings have little Spirit in them, take it away, and
add to it a little Water. Put fome of it into a-long
flender Phial, and fhake it brifkly, or give it a ftroke
upon your Hand; obferve the Bubbles at the Top of
the Liquor, they fhould be moderately large, and
ftand a good while; when they are large and go off
quick, and the Liquor is perfectly clear, it is too
ftrong and requires a little more Water; but let this
be put in gently, and by fmall Quantities, till the
Head ftands a long Time: If too much Water be put
in, the Bubbles will be fmall, and go off quick, and
the Liquor will not be fo clear.

This is beft tried in a fmall Quantity in the Phial
firft, that it may be perfectly underftood, and then it
will be eafy to bring the whole to a right Strength.

When it is too ftrong a little more Water brings it
down; and when too much, if fuch a Thing happen,
by putting in the Water too haftily, then it is only to
be remembered every Time it is ufed: A little more
of it is to be put into the Still than is ordered in the
Receipt, and the Water will be of a proper Strength,
as if the Spirit had been ever fo right before.

C H A P. III.

Spirit of Wine.

WE have fhewn what is meant by Spirit of Wine,
that is a Spirit twice a ftrong as Brandy, and
which on being fet on Fire, will all burn away: This
is what is called All-hot, and it is thus made.

Put a Gallon of the Proof Spirit made as before
directed into a Still, and make a fmall Fire under it,
diftil off two Quarts, or a very little lefs than that
Quantity, and it is what we mean by Spirit of Wine.
Set it by for the Ufes directed hereafter. Having thus
fhewn the Nature of the different Kinds of Spirit,

and

and directed thofe who pleafe to make them, and others to buy them properly, for the feveral Purpofes, we fhall proceed to their Ufe in the feveral Compofitions, perfixing this general Caution to the Buyers, that Proof Spirits fhould never be accepted but when it anfwers to the Defcription of the Head ; and that Spirit of Wine is not of a due Strength unlefs it will all burn away.

C H A P. IV.

Of Cordial Waters.

A R T. I. *Wormwood Water.*

CHUSE fome frefh and fine Seville Oranges, peel them thin, and take of the fine yellow Rind thus pared frefh, four Ounces ; cut it fine and put it into a Still ; bruife four Ounces of Cinnamon, and put to it ; and add four Ounces of fine Calamus Aromaticus Root fliced alfo, and a little bruifed : Add to thefe frefh Leaves of Roman Wormwood half a Pound, and Tops of Spearmint four Ounces ; cut an Ounce of Mace fmall with Sciffars, and bruife an Ounce of the leffer Cardamum Seeds with their Hufks ; put thefe to the reft in the Still, and pour on two Gallons of Brandy or other Proof Spirit.

Put on the Head of the Still, and clofe it round with Paper, ftop the Nofe of the Worm, and let all continue thus four Days.

Then open the Still, and put in a Gallon of Water.

Clofe it up again and make a gentle Fire ; let the Liquor warm gradually, but when it is come to work, let the Liquor be kept running in a continued Thread, till there is come over three Quarts and Half a Pint : Take this away, and add a Pint and Half of Water ; the whole will then be of the Strength of Brandy, and will make an excellent Cordial Water.

The Receipt is taken from the Edinburgh Difpenfatory, and it is worthy to be kept in every Family.

It

It is Cordial and Stomachick; excellent to chear the Spirits, and to take after any Food that has difagreed with the Stomach. It will in this Cafe take off the Sicknefs, and will prevent fainting.

We may obferve on this Water in particular, what fhould be kept in Remembrance on every other Occafion, which is that a great Part of its Virtue and Efficacy, depend upon a careful Choice of the Ingredients, and that Errors or Careleffnefs in this Refpect, rob the Medicines of their Virtues, and are much more common than is imagined.

In this particular Water there are two Ingredients frequently mifmanaged; thefe are the Roman Wormwood, and the Calamus Aromaticus.

As to the firft, a different Plant is frequently, nay commonly fold under its Name; and as to the other, the Englifh wild Kind is ufed by fome, tho' greatly inferior to the right foreign Sort.

The Apothecaries conftantly ufe the wild Sea Wormwood when Roman Wormwood is ordered; tho' this Sea Wormwood is a difagreeable Bitter, and the true Roman Kind is a fine Aromatick, as well as Stomachick. The true Roman Wormwood is very common in Gardens, but not ufed; it may always be had of the Nurferymen, and a good Root planted in Spring, will fpread over many Yards of Ground by the End of Summer, and ftand for ever. We advife the Houfekeeper to have this in her Garden, and always to ufe it when the Roman Wormwood is ordered, either in Diftillation or for Bitters.

As to the Calamus Aromaticus, it is the Root of a Kind of Flag, brought dry from warmer Countries: One Mr. Blackftone an Apothecary in Fleet-ftreet, fome Years fince difcovered that the fame Plant was wild in England in many Places, and publifhing this in a Catalogue of the Plants growing wild about *Harefield*, the Place of his Nativity, others obferved it in other Places, and the Druggifts in London are fince that Time in a great meafure fupplied from our

own

own Ditches with a Root they ufed to receive from abroad. They will favour the Cheat becaufe it comes cheaper; but a Fraud, and a very great one it is, to fell this under the Name of that Drug; for tho' the Plant be the fame, the Root is raifed to a much greater Degree of Fragrance and Virtue abroad, than in our cold Climate.

We fee the fame in Angelica, the Root of our own growth is very good frefh; but the dried Root of the Spanifh Kind is vaftly preferable; it is ten times fweeter. The Plant is the fame there and here, but the Root obtains more Virtues from the Heat.

2. *Compound Annifeed Water.*

Bruife in a large Mortar half a Pound of Annifeeds, and the fame Quantity of Angelica Seeds dried; put them into a Still, pour on them a Gallon of Proof Spirit, and three Quarts of Water. Fix on the Head, make a brifk Fire, and diftil off three Quarts and three Quarters of a Pint. Add a Pint and a Quarter of Water, and fet it by for Ufe.

This has all the Virtues of common Annifeed Water in difpelling Wind, and is befides a great Cordial.

It is alfo much pleafanter than the common Annifeed. No Water is better than this againft the Cholick, and any Sicknefs arifing from Victuals difagreeing with the Stomach; none better when going into a bad Air.

A Tea Spoonful of this Water put into half a Pint of an Infant's Victuals is very good againft the Wind, with which thofe tender Creatures are frequently tormented.

3. *Stomachick Water.*

Beat to a grofs Powder four Ounces of Vintners Bark, put this into a Still, and pour upon it a Gallon of Proof Spirit: Pare fome fine Lemons very thin, and cut to Pieces two Ounces of the Yellow Rind, add

N°. XVI. 3 Q this

this to the Ingredients in the Still, and then put in an Ounce of fmall Cardamum Seeds bruifed.

Cover up the Still, and let the whole ftand two Days; then open it, pour in three Quarts of Water, and clofing on the Head, make a moderate Fire. Diftil three Quarts and three Quarters of a Pint, and add a Pint and Quarter of Water: This is excellent againft any fudden Sicknefs, and againft that Coldnefs of the Stomach that often breeds Wind.

4. *Cardamum Water.*

Pick four Ounces of the leffer Cardamum Seeds from the Husks, bruife them a little, and put them into a Still with a Gallon of Proof Spirit, and two Quarts of Water; clofe on the Head, make the Fire, and draw off three Quarts and a Pint: Add a Pint of Water, and fet it by for Ufe.

This has the fame Virtues with the former againft Wind, and Coldnefs of the Stomach, and is ftronger to the Tafte, but not fo pleafant.

There is a Flavour in this Water like Spirit of Wine and Camphire. This appears particular to many, but it is not wonderful to thofe acquainted with the Nature of thefe Seeds: The ingenious Dr. James Parfons, who four or five Years fince publifhed an Account of various Seeds viewed by the Microfcope, a Work not received fo well as it deferved, fhewed by that curious Examination, that there is in every Seed of Cardamum, a Lump of real Camphire.

5. *Juniper Water.*

Bruife together an Ounce and Half of Carraway Seeds, and the fame Quantity of Sweet Fennel Seeds; put thefe into a Still, pour a Gallon of Proof Spirit upon them, and add a Pound of Juniper Berries whole: Laft of all, add three Quarts of Water, and then clofe the Head of the Still.

Make a moderate Fire, and draw off three Quarts and a Pint, and add a Pint of Water; mix this by fhaking, and fet it by for Ufe.

This

This is Good in Flatulencies and Pains in the Stomach and Bowels, occasioned by Wind. It also operates by Urine.

6. *Nutmeg Water.*

Bruise slightly two Ounces of Nutmegs, and put them into a Still with a Gallon of Proof Spirit, and two Quarts of Water; close on the Head, make a gentle Fire and distil seven Pints; add a Pint of Water and set it by for Use. It is Cordial and Carminative, good in any sudden Sickness at the Stomach, and in Cholicks.

7. *General Rules for making Cordial Waters.*

To these several particular Receipts for Cordial Waters, we shall add some general Rules that should be always kept in Mind by the House-keeper, and will give her credit in this Respect.

The Use of French Brandy is not necessary for these Waters or any other; no Spirit is better, but those of less Expence will serve: All the Care to be taken is, that the Spirit be of a due Strength, and that it have no particular Smell or Taste of its own; because in that Case it will give them to the Water.

For this Reason Melasses Spirit is preferred, because being made of Sugar, it is without Smell, whereas Malt Spirit, which is cheaper, is very offensive: In the second Place, she must observe to let the Spirit and Ingredients stand a longer or shorter Time together, according to the Nature of those Ingredients. Such as are light and fine, as Seeds and Aromatick Herbs may be distilled immediately when put together, as the Nutmeg Water, Cardamum Water, and the like; others should stand a longer Time to draw a Tincture, as the Wormwood Water, in which there is a hard Root, and some Plants of a firmer Texture.

Thirdly this, to regulate the Fire according to the same Rule; the lighter Ingredients requiring a lesser Heat, and the firmer and heavier a greater.

In

In this fhe is to be guided by the Time it is proper to let them ftand together. Such as are to be worked off immediately, fhould have a very gentle. heat, juft fo much as to keep the Spirit running in a Thread; the others fhould have a ftronger Fire in proportion to the Time needful for their ftanding to take a Tincture : Thus in directing this time of ftanding, the other is implied without farther Care or Repetition.

Laftly, fhe is to obferve never to draw off fo much as the Spirit that was put on, but to make up the diftilled Liquor to that Quantity with Water. All Vegetables have two Kinds of Oils in them, a finer and a coarfer ; the finer is all that fhould rife in the Cordial Water, the other is naufceous. This fine Oil always rifes firft, and the other never till the faint Part of the Spirit, which has itfelf alfo a difagreeable Flavour arifing from the Oil of the Spirit wherewith it is made ; thefe two ill Taftes coming together, are the utter deftruction of the Water in Point of Elegance.

This Caution is the more needful to be given, becaufe it is continually tranfgreffed in the Country Diftillations, and by too many Apothecaries; they think they fhall lofe a Part of their Quantity, if they do not let it run to the laft Drop of the Spirit ; and therefore they take in the Faints of the Still, and the coarfe Oil of the Plant ; but this is a Miftake, for they will have the fame Quantity of the diftilled Liquor, and of the fame Strength, if they give over the Diftillation in Time, and fill up to the Quantity with Water.

Some Ingredients bear diftilling farther than others without fending up their coarfe Oil ; and this we have from repeated Experience brought into Practice, in the different Receipts here delivered ; having ordered more to be drawn from fuch as are not ready to fend up this difagreeable Oil, and lefs from fuch as are ; the Water being afterwards added to make up in a

pro-

proportioned Quantity, fo as to bring all to the fame Strength at laft.

This is a Thing for which no general Rule can be given, it is only to be learned from Experience, and we therefore hope we have in this particular been of Ufe to the Diftiller of every Denomination, in fetting down the Refult of our an Experience. All Cordial Waters may be fweetened if the Maker pleafe, and in general it anfwers two good Purpofes ; it exalts the Flavour of the Ingredients, and makes the Water fine the fooner. The Quantity of Sugar may be at the Pleafure of the Houfe-keeper, two, three, or four Ounces to a Gallon.

Some think they have a great Secret in fining their Cordial Waters, which they do by Whites of Eggs, Ifinglafs, and other Ingredients, but this fpoils them in a great Meafure, and where the Art of Diftillation is underftood, according to the Rules we have laid down, it is altogether needlefs.

Cordial Waters never are foul, but when they are drawn too low or weak : Let this therefore be avoided. The proper Strength is this, that the fame Quantity of Water be made as there was of Spirit ufed ; and where this is not drawn down from the Still, but made up with about an eighth Part of Water, the whole will prefently be clear and fine. Some will look a little pearly or whitifh at firft, but the Sugar being put in, and the Bottle fet by for a Week or ten Days, the whole will be as clear as the pureft Rock Water.

The Tafte of a Cordial Water is always influenced by the Clearnefs or Foulnefs; when it is perfectly clear there is a Finenefs and Cleannefs in the Tafte, and it is pleafant ; but in proportion as it is thick or cloudy, it always taftes foul.

S E C T.

C H A P. II.

Of Simple Waters.

A R T. I. *Mugwort Water.*

CUT fmall three Pounds of the frefh Leaves and Tops of Mugwort, put them into a Still with two Gallons and a half of Water, let them ftand all Night, and the next Morning diftil off a Gallon.

This is not a pleafant Water, but it is excellent againft Hyfterick Complaints of all Kinds. A Quarter of a Pint is to be taken at a Time.

2. *Calamint Water.*

Cut fmall the whole Herb Calamint, weigh two Pounds and a half of it, put this into a Still with two Gallons of Water, and after ftanding all Night draw off a Gallon,

This is another of the Waters that are good in Hyfterick Complaints; it promotes the Menfes, difpels Wind, and is excellent in Cholicks.

3. *Water of Dill Seeds.*

Take a Pound of the Seeds of Dill frefh dried, bruife them in a Mortar, and put them into a Still with two Gallons of Water; diftil off one Gallon. This is good againft the Cholick, and in all Flatulencies.

The beft Way of giving the Simple Waters, is mixed with the Cordial ones; the right Proportion being fix Ounces of the Simple and two of the Cordial Water, which, fweetened with Sugar, or any cordial Syrup, makes a pleafant and wholfome Julep.

This is the beft and moft wholfome Way of ufing the Cordial as well as the Simple Waters, and from doing otherwife many who have taken the latter at firft as Medicines, have got into a Habit afterwards of drinking them as Drams, from which they never were able to break themfelves.

S E C T.

S E C T. VI.

Of Diforders and their Remedies.

THIS laft Obfervation on the proper Ufe of Cordial and Simple Waters naturally leads into the Ufe of other Medicines, and to the Confideration of thofe Diforders to which they are appropriated: In this, as in the former Articles, we fhall endeavour to be ufeful and plain, avoiding all obfcure Words, and all uncertain Accounts of the Virtues of Medicines; the Health of the Reader is too important a Matter to be trifled with, either through Careleffnefs or the Oftentation of ufelefs and idle Learning.

ART. I. *Againft a violent Purging er Bloody-Flux.*

Mix together fix Drams of burnt Hartfhorn and three Drams of levigated Crabs Eyes, put them into a Saucepan with three Pints of Water; add frefh Roots of Comfrey and frefh Roots of Tormentil, of each two Drams; boil away a Pint, and then ftrain off the Liquor; pour it into a Quart Bottle thick, and add to it two Ounces of fmall Cinnamon Water, and an Ounce of Syrup of Diacodium.

This is to be fhook up every Time it is taken. A Tea Cup full is the proper Dofe, and it is an excellent Remedy when the Stools are fo frequent that there is fcarce any Intermiffion, and fo fharp that they feem to cut the Paffages.

This Medicine, at two or three Times taking, allays the Pain, and brings them toward a Stop. It may be taken once in three Hours, and the beft Time for each Dofe is juft after a Stool. When they are lefs frequent the Medicine is lefs wanted.

2. *For*

2. *For a common Loofenefs.*

Set on three Ounces of the Rafpings of Logwood, and two Quarts of Water, to boil for half an Hour; toward the End of that Time break in two Drams of Cinnamon ; then fet it by to cool, firft ftraining it off.

This is a fafe and excellent Aftringent in common Cafes. A Tea Cup full is to be taken four Times a Day.

3. *For a Swelling.*

Cut a Handful of the Leaves of Mallows very fmall, put them into a Saucepan with two Quarts of Water ; add Elder Flowers, Camomile Flowers, and Melilot Flowers, of each half an Ounce, and of Fen-nigreek Seeds one Ounce ; boil thefe together a Quarter of an Hour ; then ufe it outwardly as a Fomentation, wetting Flannels in it warm, and applying them to the Swelling one after another as they cool.

4. *For the Gravel.*

Take Roots of Mallows, Reft Harrow, and Liquorice, of each half an Ounce, Seeds of wild Carrot and Linefeed, of each three Drams, put them into three Quarts of Water, and fet them over the Fire ; add four Figs cut in Slices, and two Ounces of ftoned Raifins ; boil them half an Hour, then ftrain off the Liquor, and let it fettle for Ufe.

A Quarter of a Pint is to be taken once in three Hours till the Patient have Relief. It will take off any Inflammation in the Parts, and bring away Gravel or fmall Stones.

5. *For a Cough.*

Take Barley, Figs, and Raifins, of each two Ounces, Liquorice half an Ounce, and Florentine Iris Root half an Ounce ; put the Iris Root and Barley into two Quarts of Water, and boil them well ; then put in the Raifins, Figs, and Liquorice, let it boil up again, and after eight or ten Minutes ftrain it off.

This

This is pleafanter than the Decoction directed in a former Number for the fame Purpofe, and in common tickling Coughs will very well anfwer the Purpofe. A Coffee Cup full is a Dofe, and is to be taken twice a Day.

6. *Againft malignant Fevers.*

Put into a Saucepan a Pint of Water, put in three Drams of Powder of the Bark, and the fame Quantity of Virginian Shakeroot; boil it till but Half a Pint remains, ftrain this off, and add to it an Ounce and Half of ftrong Cinnamon Water, and two Drams of Syrup of Clove July Flowers.

The Dofe is a fmall Tea Cup full every fix Hours.

The great Danger of malignant Fevers is toward the Crifis, and this Medicine is of vaft Service at that Time; it operates as a Cordial and a Sweat; and when a Perfon is recovered by this Means, it is very proper to repeat the Medicine to prevent a Relapfe.

7. *A bitter Infufion.*

Cut into thin Slices Half an Ounce of Guilian Root, the fame Quantity of the Peel of Seville Oranges or of Lemons, and of the Tops of fmall Centaury two Drams; pour upon thefe in a Stone Jar a Pint of Water boiling hot, and let it ftand till cold; then pour it off through a Sieve.

Let a Tea Cup full of this be taken every Morning fafting. It is excellent to prevent Sicknefs of the Stomach, and give an Appetite.

It fhould be taken for a Continuance of Time, and it will do Service in all Obftructions.

8. *Againft the Scurvy.*

Cut to Pieces two Ounces of the dried Leaves of Buckbeans or Marfh Trefoil, and Half an Ounce of frefh Orange Peel; pour on thefe two Quarts of boiling Water, let it ftand till it is cold, and then ſtrain it off; add to it four Ounces of compound Horſeradiſh Water; and let the Patient take a Quarter of a Pint Morning and Night for a Continuance of Time, for the Effect is not ſpeedy.

9. *Againſt Diſorders of the Head.*

Cut to Pieces two Ounces of wild Valerian Root, and an Ounce of the Leaves of Sage freſh gathered; pour on theſe two Quarts of boiling Water, and let it ſtand till it is cold; then ſtrain it off.

Let the Patient take a Quarter of a Pint of it twice a Day, and continue it for ſome Time.

It is excellent againſt Pains, Giddineſs, and all Diſorders of the Head, and is good in all nervous Caſes.

RECEIPTS *from* Lady Hewet's *Book.*

1. *A Powder for the Teeth.*

TAKE burnt Allum, Maſtick, Bole Armoniack, and Dragons Blood, of each Half an Ounce, finely beaten and ſearced. You may add Leaf Gold to it if you pleaſe.

2. *A Powder for an intermitting Fever.*

Take the Roots of Virginian Snakeweed powdered, and of the Powder of Crabs Eyes or Coral, each Half a Scruple; mix them, and take this Powder in a Spoon, with a little of the following Julep, and drink five or ſix Spoonfuls of the Julep after it.

The Julep.

Take of Fever Milk and Balm Water each Half a Pint, of black Cherry Water a Quarter of a Pint, of Barley Cinnamon Water three Ounces, and of Syrup of Lemon two Ounces; mix them together, and keep it in a Bottle for Uſe.

Take

Take of this Powder and Julep the Quantities above directed as foon as the Fit is wholly off, and the fame Quantity once in four Hours during the Intermiffion, if the Fever be violent; if it be moderate, the taking three or four Dofes Night and Morning will be enough.

3. *Steel Pills.*

Take three Drams of Steel, three Drams of Saffron, three Drams of Alloes, and three Drams of Rhubarb, make thefe into Pills with Syrup of Rofes, and take four every Night going to Bed, with a Draught of fomething warm after them, and fomething warm alfo in the Morning that is not made with Milk; if it is Water Gruel put a little Wine in it.

The Apothecary may make them large, and then three will ferve. They fhould work two or three Times in a Day, or elfe you muft take another.

4. *For the Green Sicknefs.*

Take two Pennyworth of prepared Steel, two Pennyworth of Alloes, and one Pennyworth of Liquorice, all in Powder. It is to be made up in Pills if you pleafe, or in the Powder, if you like that beft. It is to be divided into nine Dofes, one of which muft be taken every Morning; after which you muft reft nine Days, and then take it again. Do this till well.

5. *For the fame.*

Take of the beft Honey four Ounces, Conferve of Damafk Rofes two Ounces, prepared Steel an Ounce and a half, and Powder of Ginger an Ounce; mix thefe together, and take the Quantity of a Nutmeg Night and Morning, drinking a Glafs of Wine after it.

6. *For the fame.*

Take a Pound of blue Currants rubbed clean, but not wafhed, put them into a Quart of Lifbon white Wine in a Jar that you may the eafier come at it; keep it clofe ftopped up, and after two Days you may take it.   A Spoonful of the Currants and Liquor together is to be taken every Morning; and when it is half exhaufted you may add another Pint of Wine to the Remainder of the Currants, and fo on till you have taken the whole.

7. *For the Scurvy or Green Sicknefs.*

Take four Quarts of white Wine and two Quarts of Broom Afhes, a Shillingfworth of Saffron, and a Lemon cut full of Holes; tie the Afhes and Saffron up in a Bag, and put it into the Wine with the Lemon; let it ftand thus three or four Days and it will be fit for Ufe.   Six Spoonfuls is a Dofe, which muft be repeated three or four Times a Day.

8. *For a Stoppage of the Courfes by a Cold.*

Take as much Powder of Myrrh as a Spoon will hold, mix it with Poffet Ale, and give a Draught of it as hot as it can be drank; this will lay the Patient in a Sweat. Boil in the Poffet-Drink Camomile, Pennyroyal, and Mugwort, of each a like Quantity, ftrain it very clear, fweeten it, and give the Patient two Quarts in two Hours; this will continue the Sweat. If the Body be bound put up a Suppofitory, which is to be made thus:

Take a Spoonful of Honey and a little Salt, mix thefe together upon a Trencher, and when it is ftiff enough roll them into long fmall Rolls, fharper at one End than the other.   I have ufed this Medicine with great Succefs.

9. *Dr. Wright's Red Water for bringing down the Courfes, or quickening Throes in Labour.*

Take a Quart and Half a Pint of Aqua Vitæ, put into it two Drams of Hira Picra, ftop it clofe, and let it ftand in the Sun or by the Fire fourteen Days, fhaking it twice a Day; then ftrain it off, and put to it two Drams of the Powder of Liquorice; let it ftand fix Days longer, fhaking it as before.

To a Woman in Travel give a Spoonful, or a Spoonful and a Half if Need requires.

It

To Maids it fhould be given in Sanctuary or Penny-royal Water: Three Drams of the Powder is fuffi-cient to a Quart of Water. Take fix Spoonfuls in a Morning, fafting two Hours after it.

10. *To caufe eafy Labour.*

Ten or twelve Days before you look take fix Ounces of brown Sugar-candy beaten to Powder, a Quarter of a Pound of Raifins ftoned, two Ounces of Dates un-ftoned and fliced, Half an Ounce of Annifeeds bruifed, à Quarter of an Ounce of Cowflip Flowers, and one Dram of Rofemary Flowers; tie thefe up in a fine Lawn Bag, and put them into a Bottle of white Wine, with a Flint Stone tied to it to make it fink; let it fteep twenty-four Hours, then take of it in the Morn-ing, at four o'Clock in the Afternoon, and in the Evening, the Quantity of a Wine Glafs full.

11. *A Powder for a Woman in Extremity in Travel.*

Take white Amber, Cinnamon, and Date Stones, of each a like Quantity in fine Powder; give as much at a Time as will lie upon a Shilling in a Spoonful of warm Caudle.

12. *Another for the fame.*

Take feven Bay Berries, beat them to Powder, and mix with them an equal Quantity of Cinnamon and white Amber: Give this in Extremity, when all Things are right.

13. *For a Loofenefs in a Woman in Childbed.*

Take a Pint of new Milk and feeth it, let it ftand till it be no warmer than Milk from the Cow, then put into it two Yolks of Eggs well beaten, and a Spoonful of Loaf Sugar.

14. *For a Woman that cannot be cleared of the Secun-dine after the Birth of a Child.*

Mix a Pennyworth of Mummy in three or four Spoonfuls of white Wine Poffet, and give it the Wo-man to drink.

15. *Dr.*

15. *Dr. Myron's Receipt to ſtrengthen a Woman after Travel, if in Pain.*

Take Pomegranate Buds, red Roſe Leaves, and the Bark of Oak, of each a like good Quantity, and boil them in Spring Water till it be a ſtrong Decoction; then to a Pint of this put a Quarter of a Pint of red Wine, dip a Rag double in it, and apply to the Part as warm as you can well ſuffer it; cloſe up the Body with it, and keep it up with double Clouts; do this every Night a good while together, keeping it on all Night.

Put Aſafœtida into an earthen Pot upon a few Embers, and ſit over the Smoke; this will drive it up at firſt.

16. *Againſt Miſcarriage.*

Take a Nutmeg groſsly beaten, Mace, Cloves, and Cinnamon, of each the Quantity of a Nutmeg, groſsly beaten likewiſe; put them into a little Cotton, and the Cotton into a ſcarlet Silk Bag, with a few Camomile Flowers; tie it round the Waſte next the Skin, and let it lie down behind to the Hollow of the Back.

SECT. VII.

Of the Diſorders of Cattle, and their Remedies.

NO Part of the Family Concern in the Country is ſo little underſtood as the proper Management of Cattle; the Care of them is in general committed to ignorant and conceited Perſons, and they are more deſtructive to the Creatures than all their Diſorders.

We ſhall hope to ſet this Matter upon the ſame clear Footing with the reſt, and that every Reader
will

will be his own Judge how to proceed, or to know how thofe proceed to whom he commits the Care of his fick or hurt Cattle of whatever Kind.

C H A P. I.

Of Horfes.

A RT. I. *For watery, blood-fhot, or inflamed Eyes.*

CUT a Handful of the Leaves of Wormwood, and the fame Quantity of the Leaves of Betany, bruife them in a Mortar, and add to them half a Spoonful of Ox's Gall ; pound them well together, and prefs out the Juice ; with this rub the Eye all over gently and carefully every Night and Morning.

I have feen very great Cures performed by this fometimes in two Days ; but if it be not fo fudden it is fure, and the beft Way is to continue it from Day to Day till it take Effect, which is rarely above five or fix Days.

Different Beafts will have the fame Diforder in various Degrees, therefore fome Difference is required in the treating it.

If the Malady be very ftubborn, the Eye much inflamed, and the Medicine take no Effect in two or three Days ufing, let him be blooded, and continue to ufe the Medicine, and he will foon be well.

2.   *For the Vives.*

What Farriers in the Country call the Vives is a Swelling and Inflamation of the Glands, which fome call the Kernels between the Neck and the Chaps.

Beat a large Handful of Rue in a Mortar, and pour to it three Spoonfuls of Vinegar ; prefs out the Juice ; mix with this a large Houfe Spoonful of Pepper, and the fame Quantity of melted Hogs Lard.

Stir all this together that it may be perfectly mixed, and then divide it into two Parts ; put one into each Ear of the Horfe, and tie them in.

Then

Then let the Horſe be blooded moderately, and turned into the Stable.

This is a Remedy at once; it ſeldom needs any Repetition, eſpecially if the Diſorder be taken in Time.

3. *For Wind Galls.*

Wind Galls are ſoft Swellings that come on each Side the Fetlock; they generally are cauſed by long Journies on hard Roads: They are very troubleſome to the Horſe, but the Cure is eaſy.

Let them be cut open and cleanſed, then put a Plaiſter of common Pitch over them. Let it hang till it drop off.

C H A P. II.

Of Oxen and Cows.

A R T. I. *Of the Fever.*

THE larger horned Cattle are ſubject to an abſolute and regular Fever, which is often deſtructive to them in a few Days, and at other Times hangs upon them, and prevents their thriving.

The Signs to know it are theſe: They tremble firſt, and afterwards grow reſtleſs and unquiet; they will not eat, they lie and roll upon the Ground, they foam at the Mouth and groan, and their Fleſh is very hot.

The firſt Thing is to bleed the Beaſt largely, then give the following Medicine:

Bruiſe the Roots of Maſterwort, and expreſs their Juice; take a Quarter of a Pint of this, a Quart of Ale, and a Houſe Spoonful of Mithridate; boil them up together, and when cool enough give it to the Creature.

Let this be repeated twice a Day, and if the Diſorder do not abate on the third Day let the Beaſt be blooded more largely than before, and continue the ſame Medicine.

The

The Creature will be weak when it firſt recovers, but that will ſoon go off. I have ſeen a Cow cured by this Medicine when ſhe lay ſtruggling in the Field, and the Crows were watching about her ready to fall to their Prey.

The Food, as the Creature recovers, ſhould be the fineſt Hay ſprinkled with Water; after that it is by Degrees to be brought to good ſweet Graſs.

2. *For the Murrain.*

Mix together a Pint and a Half of Wine which has ſtood ſeveral Days, and two Ounces of Hens Dung; give it the Beaſt every Evening for four Times, or more if needful.

This is a plain ſimple Remedy, but it is not without great Power: Both the Ingredients abound in a volatile Salt, which will have great Effects in this Diſorder, and Experience ſhews that it is a noble Remedy.

Perhaps, after all the vain Attempts to remedy the great and terrible Diſtemper that has ſo many Years raged among the horned Cattle, by Chemical Medicines, this homely Remedy may take Effect.

We have not had Opportunities of bringing it into Trial in this Reſpect, but have ſeen ſo much Good from it in other Caſes that ſeem not very different, that we cannot but wiſh to ſee it fairly tried in this.

C H A P. III.

Of Sheep.

A R T. I. *Againſt Worms.*

SHEEP are ſubject to Worms in their Bowels, and are greatly tortured with them.

They are known to have this Complaint by a heavy Look in their Eyes, a frequent Itching of their Noſes, ſo that they rub them againſt any Thing, and by their lying upon their Side and kicking their Belly with their Feet.

In this Cafe bruife fome Leaves of **Wormwood**, prefs out the Juice, and give the Sheep a Quarter of a Pint of it early in the Morning when its Stomach is moft empty, and make the Creature ftir about, and keep it from Food for fome Time afterwards. Repeat this feveral Days and the Cure will be certain, all the Symptoms will vanifh, and the Sheep will feed and be eafy.

2. *For the Rot.*

This is the moft terrible of all Diforders to Sheep, and when it takes place often becomes in a Manner univerfal.

The beft Remedy is this : Mix Half an Ounce of Powder of Elecampane and four Ounces of Bay Salt dried and rubbed to Powder, divide this into fix Dofes, and give one every Morning to the Sheep that begin to droop.

Not only Experience fhews the good Effect of this, but it is confirmed alfo by other Inftances.

No Sheep die of the Rot in falt Marfhes, therefore the Salt is able to prevent this Complaint, and with the Affiftance of the Elecampane, which is itfelf a very powerful Remedy, it entirely cures it.

3. *Of the different Herbs that are good or bad for Sheep.*

We have delivered the Remedies for fome of the principal Diforders to which Sheep are liable in this and the preceding Months, but we fhall not think the Rules for the Cure of this tender and ufeful Animal compleated till we have given proper Directions for their Prefervation.

Many of the Diforders of Sheep are owing to the Herbs that grow in their Paftures. Nature has given every Animal a Direction of Inftinct for the avoiding fuch Plants as are abfolutely poifonous ; but there are others which, though they have not the full and immediate

mediate Effect of Poifons, yet bring on Diforders which in the End deftroy the Creature : Againft thefe Inftinct does not fo ftrongly guard Animals, and the Sheep, more remarked for its Meeknefs than its Cunning, often falls a Prey to this flow Deftruction.

Now what the Sheep has not the Difcretion to diftinguifh the Shepherd fhould, and that he may perfectly know how to do this we fhall lay him down the plaineft Information, according to the Names and Nature of the Plants, all of which are common, and fufficiently known.

The Farmer will alfo do well to examine into this himfelf, and to obferve what Herbs are the Product of his Grounds among the Grafs, that he may propagate fuch as are healthful, and root out fuch as are hurtful.

His Care will be very well rewarded by the thriving of his Sheep, and the Shepherd's Credit will always rife in Proportion to his Caution in keeping them from what is left of a dangerous Kind, and encourageing them to feed where there are the more wholfome Kinds.

Firft then, the Herbs moft wholfome and healthful for Sheep are thefe : White Trefoil, Selfheal, Pimpernel, wild Clover, Melilot, and Cinquefoil ; and to thefe may be added wild Thyme, called Mother of Thyme, and Broom.

The former Kinds are common in many Paftures, and the latter on hilly Grounds in fome Degree barren.

The former will always keep Sheep well, and the others will frequently recover them from their Diforders.

Therefore to keep thefe Creatures in Health let thefe feveral Herbs be encouraged.

Melilot produces a deal of Seed, and it is eafy to gather this and fcatter it about the Hedges, where it will fpring up of itfelf; the others will take Care of themfelves, and fpread wherever they are undifturbed.

When

When any Diforder appears in the Flock the Shepherd is to drive them to thofe hilly Paftures where Broom and wild Thyme grow: They will crop the Tops of the Broom, and lightly bite the wild Thyme, and its very aromatick Smell will cure them as they lie among it.

Thefe are not Paftures on which to fatten Sheep, but when they have throve but indifferently upon the richeft Grounds let them be kept a few Days upon thefe, and they will then thrive on the others quickly: The Diforder that prevented their eating will thus be removed, and they will feed freely and happily upon rich Pafture.

In this Cafe the Shepherd is to act as a Phyfician to his Flock, and this is the principal Opportunity he will have of fhewing his Skill in their Management.

The Herbs hurtful to Sheep are thefe: Spearwort, which is a Kind of Water Crowfoot; Water Dropwort, which has a Flower like Hemlock; and Pennywort, which has a round Leaf growing fingly upon a long flender Stalk: This is the worft of all, and is called White Rot.

The other two are more confpicuous, becaufe larger; this runs among the Grafs and is unfeen, except faught for with a very careful Eye.

As to the Spearwort, there is no extirpating it, becaufe it creeps at the Root: The Ground may be cleared of the others.

The Farmer muft be cautious how he fuffers his Sheep to come into Fields where thefe Herbs grow; and when that cannot be avoided, the Shepherd is to obferve their Place of Growth, which is generally about Waters, and to keep the Sheep from that Part of the Ground.

Every one at all concerned about Sheep knows how injurious thofe Paftures are to them, which are fubject to frequent and repeated Overflowings: They fall into the Rot more in thefe than in any other Places:

The

The Caufe has been fought in the too abundant Moifture; but it is not that a little more or a little lefs Water is capable of taking that Effect; it is the Herbs it produces. Whenever Lands are thus fre-quently overflowed, this Herb Pennywort is ready to grow. We have obferved how eafily it efcapes the Eye, by its low and creeping Manner of growth, and this is the Caufe of the Mifchief.

To thefe Plants which are always deftructive of Sheep, we are to add two farther Cautions to the Farmer or the Shepherd, which are, that the Herb Knotgrafs, tho' not fo fatal as the others, is un-wholefome; and that the common Grafs when Mil-dewed, an Accident not uncommon in damp Places, is always hurtful.

The Caution againft thefe is not to be fo ftrict as concerning the others; but ftill it is good to be upon ones guard againft every Thing that can do Injury: A few Bites of thefe may do no Harm, but full Feeding on them will.

S E C T. VII.

Of the Management of the Garden in the Month of May.

THIS is a Month where the Sun has a great deal of Power, and if there happen fome Rain, as there generally does, efpecially towards the beginning of it; a great deal of Care muft be taken in every Quarter to keep down Weeds. The ufeful Crops will be at this Time growing ftoutly; but if they be not Cleaned from Weeds, their Progrefs will be checked, and they will be backward and poor.

This

This is all the Care required for the Crops, which will ferve in the preceding Months, and are now advancing toward Bearing: But this is not all the Gardiners Care in this Month, there are many Things he is to continue fowing which he began the former Month; fome which he may not get into the Ground tho' that Seafon were the properer, if Neglect or Accident have left the Garden hitherto without them; and befide thefe, there are fome which it is only now the proper Time for fowing.

Our Springs in England are too cold for many of the ufeful Plants of our Gardens, they muft therefore be fown in the beginning of Summer; and there are others which require the Affiftance of Hot-Beds in the earlier Months, that may now be advantageoufly fown in the naked Ground.

Upon thefe feveral Reafons, the Gardiner is to proceed in the Article of Sowing this Month, that he may have Succeffion and Variety.

He is to continue fowing all the Kinds of young Salleting: They fhould be fown once a Week, or oftener, for they grow quickly too large for Ufe.

As to their Situation, that fhould be now juft the contrary to what it was to be early in Spring; then they require a warm South Afpect, becaufe the Cold of the Seafon will elfe prevent their Growth, but now they fhould be fet in a Northern Border, for the Seafon favours them fo much, that they will foon grow fit for Ufe any where, and if they be not ftopped in fome Degree by this Method, they will very foon grow too big.

This is a very good Seafon for Endive: Let it be fown for Blanching, and let the Border be mellow, and well watered for the Reception of the Seed. It will foon be up, and then let it be carefully managed: Firft it is to be thined, for it will rife too thick; and afterwards it muft be kept very free from Weeds, for it is eafily choaked.

Purflain

Purflain may now be fown upon a good warm South Border in a fheltered Place. This Herb is too much negle&ted ; it is wholefome as well as agreeable to the Palate, and where fown at this Time, requires no Care or Trouble.

If you intend to have late Crops of Beans, fow fome the third Week in May, upon the coldeft and dampeft Border of the Garden, and Water them at Times.

Peafe may be fown for the fame Purpofe, in the fame Manner : Thefe latter will not yield a great Quantity, but their Produce will come in fo late, that the Peafe will be almoft as great a Rarity as early, and they will be full as good.

Chufe out a good rich and moderately warm Border for a fecond Sowing of Kidney Beans, and fow the Dutch Kind ; every Shop has them. Thefe are to be fown at greater Diftances in the Rows than the others, and to be kept carefully Weeded ; they will yield abundantly.

Look to the Borders where you fowed Cabbages and Celeri the foregoing Month ; the Plants will now be of a height to remove, and this muft be done. Let the Ground be well prepared for them, and if there come no Rain for the three or four firft Days, water them.

Toward the End of May 'twill be proper to prepare a Bed for Winter Cauliflowers. Sow the Seed very carefully, and defend it from Birds.

The Cucumber and Melon Plants will now require a great deal of Care ; the Sun will be fo ftrong in the middle of the Day, that they muft be defended from it, or they will flag and droop. The Evaporation from the Leaves and Stalks of fo large Plants is very great, under fo ftrong a Sun as is at this Time ; and thefe Plants raifed Artificially, have not the full Refource of thofe which fpread at random in the Earth, to draw in a due Quantity of Nourifhment to fupply the Lofs.

They

They muft be covered with Mats, and at the fame Time hardened to the Air, by raifing the Frames, and fetting the Bell-Glaffes upon Brick-bats.

A great deal of Nicety is requifite juft at this Time, in the Management of thefe Plants; for their Bearing and Continuance, will in a great Meafure depend upon it.

Notwithftanding the Heat in the Middle of the Day, there are often Frofts in the Night at this Time, and thefe will be fatal if the Plants are Expofed to them; therefore the careful Gardiner muft watch the Weather, and manage accordingly: Air the Plants muft have at this Seafon, and the more they have without Danger the better, but it is very eafy by a little Mifmanagement to deftroy them all.

The Lettuces of feveral Kinds will now demand the Gardiners nice Care in their Management.

He is to remember that befides the prefent Crop, he muft have a Succeffion; and in order to this, while he is continually drawing fome for Ufe, he muft be fowing and tranfplanting others.

The Tranfplanting in this Cafe is not as on moft other Occafions, intended to forward, but to backen the Plants.

They are growing up too faft, and the Lettuce is a Plant that does not remain long in its Perfeétion; therefore a good Number fhould now be removed, for the ftopping them; thefe fhould be fet pretty clofe in the Northern Borders, and they will thus come into Ufe after the other are eaten or grown off.

While this is doing for a Second, the Sowing is intended for a third Crop.

For this Purpofe a moderately large Bed muft be prepared by good digging, and carefully levelling the Earth. This fhould be in a Southern Expofure, and the ground rich and not exhaufted; for the fame Pains muft be taken to bring thefe forward; as to keep the other back.

The

The Seeds muſt be ſcattered thin upon this Bed, and when the Plants are come up, they muſt be carefully thinned, by taking up the Weakeſt. The proper Way is to have them at about eight Inches diſtance every Way, for they are not to be tranſplanted. The Weeds muſt be hoed from among them, and the Lettuces grow up where they riſe.

Towards the End of this Month the Gardiner muſt look over every Part of his Ground, ſee all clean, and that all goes on regularly ; he muſt obſerve that his tranſplanted Things do not fade for want of Water, and where the early Cauliflowers begin to ſhew the firſt Rudiments of a Head, he muſt break down two or three of the innermoſt Leaves over them, to cover the Flower. This will preſerve it white and make it grow thick and hard.

In the ſame Manner let the careful Gardiner look over his early Cabbages ; they will begin to round, and he will greatly aſſiſt this, by tying the top Leaves together with a Piece of old Baſs ; this has the ſame Effect upon the Cabbage, with the breaking in the Leaves upon the Cauliflower, it makes it have a better Head, and be whiter and harder.

We have mentioned that the Artichoke Suckers are now in Seaſon ; the Gardiner muſt pull them off whether the Cook require them or not, for they will come to nothing themſelves, and they will deſtroy the main Fruit. All the Nouriſhment ſhould be directed to this, that it may be tender, full of Juice, and fine ; and there is no Way of doing it, but by cutting off theſe others, which would drain it to themſelves.

The Middle of May is a very good Seaſon for ſowing of Turneps and Brocoli.

The chief Care about the Turneps is to ſee that the Seed be new, and to defend it from Birds.

Some who fear the Fly, which is ſo deſtructive to Turneps, in the young Leaf, mix their Seed half New and half Old, and this is a very good Method ;

N°. XVII.   3 R   for

for the new Seed coming up feveral Days before the
old, there are two Crops ; fo that if one be deftroyed, the other has a Chance to efcape.

When the Turneps come up they fhould be thined,
till they ftand about a Foot afunder every Way, and
thus they will thrive furprizingly, efpecially if there
happen to be a little Rain.

This frequently proves the firft Crop of Turneps in
the Garden ; thofe fown earlier come to Table in
their Courfe, and thefe have Time to ftand for a due
Growth. They muft be kept clear of Weeds afterwards, and no farther Care is required for them.

It is in the End of May the Gardiner is to prepare for the Girkin Cucumbers which are to be
pickled.

The Plants for this Ufe fhould be fown in the
naked Ground, and left to take their Chance : There
will be fome very well tafted Cucumbers upon them.

All Kinds of Ever Greens may be very well
Planted at this Seafon. They will grow very well
from Slips carefully taken off, and planted in a
good Piece of Ground : The beft is a Border towards the North ; and they muft be watered and
fheltered till they have taken Root.

The annual Aromatick Plants are now to be fown ;
fuch as Sweet Marjoram, and the like. And among
thefe it is fit we here recommend to the Gardiner
one Plant of this Clafs, which we direct the Cook
frequently to ufe, this is Sweet Bafil. It will rife
now very well if fown on a very fine Border, expofed
to the South Sun.

This is a Seafon when the Houfekeeper is to begin to prepare for Diftilling.

We have told her, in treating on that Head, that all
Plants are in their fulleft Perfection of Virtue, when
they have grown up to their Height, and are budding
for Flower. Some of them will be juft in that Condition at this Seafon, and fuch the Houfekeeper,
who fhould herfelf keep a watchful Eye over that

Quarter

Quarter of the Ground, fhould direct the Gardiner to cut, whether fhe want the whole or not; all fhould be cut, for this Reafon, that all is now in Perfection, in fuch Plants as are got into this State.

When they are cut down, fhe is to diftil what Quantity fhe judges proper, and to preferve the reft by drying in this Manner.

Let her tie up the Plant in fmall Bundles, not too tight, and hang thefe at a good Diftance from one another, in an airy Garret, not againft the Walls as fome very wrongly do, but upon Lines drawn acrofs the Garret, near the Cieling, for this Purpofe.

The Plants to be cut and gathered in this Month for thefe Purpofes, are Rofemary, in the beginning of the Month. At this Time being juft full of Flower Buds about opening, frefh diftilled with the rectified Spirit, it makes excellent Hungary Water; the remainder dried, ferves many Purpofes : This is only to be cropped. The Flowering Branches being cut off in fuch Quantity as they may be wanted, and the Shrub left as little injured as may be : The other Plants are in general to be cut down clofe to the Root. This has a very good Effect, for the Seafon not being too far advanced, nor the Roots exhaufted by the Flowering and Seeding of the Plant, there foon rifes a new Shoot, that before Autumn is fpent will bear another Cutting.

Let the Houfekeeper remember that where fhe cuts Rofemary in Bud, fome of the flowering Boughs muft be left on, that the Flowers may Ripen, for Conferve, and for the feveral other Ufes for which we have named them.

Befides the Medicinal Plants which are thus to be cut up in their due Time, this Month affords alfo feveral Flowers which fhould be gathered for the fame Purpofe; Berage and Buglofs are now in full Blow, and their Flowers muft be picked to ufe frefh or dry, for the Purpofes we have named. The

Piony

Piony Flowers will alſo be in their Prime towards the End of the Month.

Many of the Plants raiſed under hot Beds, may now be planted out into warm Borders : The Capſicum and the like, will bear the Weather if the Seaſon be tolerably favourable ; but if otherwiſe, it is better to defer it ſome Days.

Where the uſeful Products have thus been regulated, let the Gardiner turn his Eye to thoſe raiſed for Amuſement and Pleaſure.

The Flowers that are now in Bloom, of the Tulip, Ranunculus and Anemony Kinds, ſhould be managed with a great deal of Care ; theſe are Flowers Nature intended for the Spring, and we are advancing apace toward Summer. If *May* be hot, the Sun will be too powerful for them.

The Floriſt who has been at the Pains to raiſe theſe tender Delicacies, where he has gone thro' the Trouble of nurſing and tending them eleven Months of the Twelve, hopes to ſee their Colours lively, and their Continuation as long as their Nature will admit ; to obtain this, he muſt guard them from the powerful Effect of the Sun. The natural Conſequence of letting the Sun at Noon ſhine full and hot upon them, is that their Colours Fade, and they quickly fall off.

We ſee the Leaves of all tender Plants droop in the powerful Sun-ſhine, and the Effect upon Flowers is of the ſame Kind.

Beſide there is this farther Reaſon why it makes them fall quickly, that the Heat tends to the Ripening of the Seeds. This is the Purpoſe of Nature in the Growth of the Plant, and all the beautiful Parts of the Flower are but ſubſervient to it : Therefore as the more Heat of the Sun comes upon the Plant, the quicker the Seed ripens ; in conſequence the quicker the Flower falls.

This is the Occaſion for the Shading them, and the Conſequence will be, that they will be twice as

hand-

handfome, and laft twice as long as they would have done if left expofed.

Take up the Tulip Roots whofe Stalks are withered, and alfo the other bulbous Plants which have flowered.

And let this be remembred for the Flower Garden, which was faid for the other; that the Weeds muft be deftroyed now, or they will be very troublefome. They muft be hoed up in all the Borders, and between, and round about all the perennial Plants. This Hoeing up and raking off the Weeds, has a double Effect: It not only takes away all the ufelefs Growths, fo as to let the Plants which are cultivated, have all the Advantage of the Ground to themfelves, but the Hoe cutting the Surface, breaks it a little, and this is always ferviceable.

Here we fhall give the Gardiner one farther Direction, refpecting the Placing and Difpofition of his Plants. They are generally fet too clofe in our Gardens: The Florift propofes to cover the Ground with the glowing Beauties of his Production; but in this he errs, for they do not fhew themfelves fo well when thus near, as they do when fomewhat diftant. All is Confufion in this Cafe; Leaves blend with Leaves, and Flowers rife among one another in fuch Manner, that the Eye does not know where to trace them.

The better Way is to give them a little Diftance, it will always add to the Beauty of a Garden, if the Mafter of it hold this for a Rule in all Plants, to have a Space of vacant Earth round every one, on every Side. This ferves as a Frame to the Picture, and being kept always perfectly clear from Weeds, the Colour which is dark and fimple, relieves the Eye from the Variety and Glare of the Flowers: And every Plant will thrive alfo a great deal the better for this, becaufe it gives an Opportunity for hoeing, and breaking the Ground.

Large

Large Plants fhould always be kept at a farther Diftance, that the Spade may come in eafily between them; this will be a prodigious Advantage; and they will thrive beyond all others.

The Hufbandman knows what vaft Advantage there is in breaking and dividing the Ground for the Service of his Crop; and the late new invented, or revived Method of Horfe-hoeing Hufbandry, brought into Ufe by Mr. Tull, fhews the great Benefit of turning up the Ground about a Crop while growing.

One Grain of Wheat has been found to yield as many Ears by this Way of Management, as twelve in the common Method of Hufbandry. The fame will be done in favour of Garden Plants by digging between them. The Spade does this Work of breaking the Ground, better than the Hoe Plow, and this he acknowledges; therefore it is fit every Gardiner find the Advantage of this Method, it will hold good in all ufeful as well as beautiful Plants, and he may be affured of this, that the Kitchen Garden as well as the Flower Garden, will be prodigioufly improved by fetting the Plants at greater Diftances; and getting the Spade between them, fo that the Ground may be turned Deep feveral Times during their Growth.

The Advantage of all Vegetation depends on this; the keeping the Earth loofe, and the encreafing the Number of fmall Roots.

Both thefe Ends are obtained by digging between the Plants: The Earth is frequently broken, and therefore is always light and fine, and the Spade cuts off every Time the Ends of the diftant and fmall Roots of the Plant, from which new ones immediately grow in great Numbers, and fpread every Way in the rich Soil for Nourifhment.

The Gardiner knows the Advantage of tranfplanting with a good Ball; and he alfo knows the good that rifes from the cutting off the Ends of the Roots in a Plant he removes to another Place: Both thefe Ends are anfwered by the digging between the Plants,

for

for the Earth all about is made fine for the Reception
of the Roots, which is all the real Caufe of the
Benefit of Tranfplanting, and at the fame Time, the
Earth round about the Root being left undifturbed in
a much larger Ball, than could be removed with it;
there is the Benefit of having a Part of the Roots
continue fixed for immediate Nourifhment. The Ends
of the Roots are alfo cut off in this by the Spade,
but in a better Manner than where it is done by a
Knife in the other Way; becaufe here it is only the
Ends of the very fmall ones, and they are the fame
inftant covered up with Earth, fo that the Air can
take no effect upon them; whereas in the other Way,
the Ends of larger Roots are cut, and tho' they be
Planted ever fo quick, the Air will damage them.

Thus much we have thought needful to fay upon a
Point which may be of the greateft Ufe and Satisfaction to the Curious, or profitable Gardiner; advifing
the bringing it into Practice, both in the Culture of
Flowers and Kitchen Plants, digging frequently round
the firft, and between the Roots of the latter; and
digging this always to a good Depth, and always
carefully breaking the Ground.

A great many of the Ornaments of the Flower
Garden are now to be fown; they muft have the
Earth well dug for the Reception of their Seeds, and
finely broke, and they muft be fown where they are
to remain. The Candytuft, dwarf Stock, dwarf
Lychnis, and feveral others of the fmaller Kind; and
the Sweet Peafe, Lupines, and Indian Crefs, which
are large and taller; they will thrive happily fown at
this Seafon, and will continue flowering late.

This alfo is the Seafon for tranfplanting the Perennial and Biennial Flowers raifed from Seed in Spring:
They will be of fome Growth by this Time, and they
are to be carefully removed to Borders, and placed
at proper Diftances, not for flowering, but for good
Nourifhment.

The

The Gardiner muft take the Opportunity of drying Weather for this, and they will immediately take Root and thrive.

They are to ftand where they are now placed till about the End of Auguft, and they will make no unpleafing Appearance by the Variety, Frefhnefs, and Beauty of their Leaves.

If the Borders in the Garden be fo well filled that there is not Room for them, they may be planetd out in a Nurfery, or on any Bed of good Earth dug for that Purpofe.

In Auguft they muft be planted where they are to remain, and they will be very ftrong for the fucceeding Year.

Hollyhocks, French Honeyfuckles, Columbines, Sweet Williams, and the like, are all beft managed in this Manner.

Toward the End of May the Florift muft have an Eye to his Carnations; thefe are to be the great Beauty of his Garden the fucceeding Part of the Seafon, and he muft prepare for their flowering fuccefsfully by fupporting them, and hoeing up all the Nourifhment to one Point.

To this Purpofe he is now to tie up the Stalks carefully, and he muft take off all the Side Buds, for if thefe were left on they would rob the principal Flowers of Nourifhment, and yet come to nothing themfelves.

The fame Care of tying up muft be ufed alfo for all the other tall Flowers, that the Wind may not have too much Power over them. Few know the great Neceffity there is for this Practice, or the great Advantage that attends it, which we fhall explain, that the Gardiner may for the future be more careful than moft are at prefent on this Article.

Every one muft know that a Plant never requires fo much Nourifhment as when it is in flower; and it is plain from Reafon, that the more Nourifhment there is received, the ftronger and finer the Flowers in this Kind of Plants will be.

The

The Nourifhment of a Plant can never come up regularly when the main Body of the Root is difturbed; and yet this is naturally the Cafe in all tall blowing Garden Flowers, when not carefully tied up.

In Nature the Plants fucceed better, becaufe the Ground is ftiffer and fadder; but in a Garden, where all is light and loofe, the Difadvantage is plain.

When a Plant has grown to two or three Feet high, and that perhaps with a bufhy Stalk, the Wind has great Power upon it, every Blaft fways and rocks it, and loofens the Root.

I have feen in many Gardens fome of thefe tall Plants in a decaying State, and upon Examination the Caufe has been found to be this: On looking at the Bottom of the Stalk there has been a Hole gulled and worn like a Funnel by the rolling of the Stalk round and round, by the Force of the Wind, and the Root has been expofed to the Air, and continually loofened. Thus has a Plant, raifed with a great deal of Care, and brought very happily juft to the Time of its flowering, drooped and decayed, and the Owner wondered, when it was only owing to this one Neglect. If the Plant had been tied up to a good ftout Stick when it firft got up into Stalk, nothing of this would have happened, the Stalk itfelf would have grown up much ftronger, becaufe better fupported, and the Wind would have had no Power to have hurt the Root by its Waves.

Having thus fhewn the Reafon and Neceffity of ftaiking or tying-up of Plants, we muft give one Caution, which is, that the Plant be not injured by the rude and unfkilful Way of doing it; let the Stick be cut very even and fharp at the End that is to go into the Ground, and let its Shape there be flatted; then take Care to thruft it carefully and fteadily into the Ground, without injuring the Roots of the Plant; it muft be thruft in deep, or it cannot be fteady, and if not perfectly fteady in itfelf it can be of no Service to the Plant; this will be beft done by thrufting it ftrait and forcibly down, and then the Care muft be not to place it too near the Stalk of the Plant, becaufe that will throw it upon the full or main Body of the Root, which it may greatly injure.

The tying being thus managed in Time, and with due Care, will be of the utmoft Service to the Plants, and the Benefit will be feen in the Frefhnefs of their Leaves, which in the Height of Summer is a great Beauty, and in the Number and Strength of the Flowers.

Toward the End of this Month the Auriculas being perfectly out of Flower fhould be removed to a fhady quiet Place, and the Stages prepared for the finer Carnations. The Pots muft be well examined, and every Thing fearched for Fear of Vermin. There is no Flower which is fo much infefted with them, or fo often deftroyed by them; and it muft be a very provoking Circumftance for the Florift to fee the Labour and Expectation of a Year or two deftroyed by a Worm.

May is a very important Month for the Management of regularly growing Fruit Trees. The Efpaliers muft be looked over, and from Time to Time all fore-right Shoots taken off, and the others that grow in a good Direction properly trained.

This is eafy now, but by a little Omiffion it will foon become very difficult, and all that might have been kept beautiful will get a Look of Wildnefs.

The Wall Fruit muft now be looked after, with Care, for it is well eftablifhed, and muft be thinned.

The Apricots will hang in vaft Clufters, and the Peaches grow together in Lumps. This is not to be permitted; they are carefully to be thinned, and in this let not the Owner be afraid of reducing his Store too far, let him thin them boldly, for it is better to have a fmall Number well ripened, large, and truly flavoured, than a Heap of ill-tafted and half ftarved ones. The common Error is letting too many of the Wall Fruit remain on, which not only hurts and

fpoils

fpoils all that fhould come to good the prefent Year, but miferably weakens the Tree for the next.

Nature in all thefe Cafes produces more than fhe intends fhould ripen; fhe provides for the Food of Infects and other Devourers, and as thefe are kept off in a great Meafure in a well-managed Garden, the Growth fhould be reduced in the fame Manner.

As to the Number of Fruit to be left upon a Tree, it muft be proportioned to the Kind of Fruit, and to the Strength of the Tree; the ftouter and more eftablifhed the Tree is, the more it will be able to nourifh and ripen, and the fmaller the Fruit the more there may be of them. Apricots may be left thicker than Peaches, becaufe they are fmaller, and remain a lefs Time upon the Tree, which is alfo a material Confideration. Large Peaches ought to be a full Span afunder upon the whole Tree; they will by this Means ripen fo finely that one will be worth half a dozen.

The Vines muft be carefully looked after, and kept in Order; fuch Shoots as have Fruit upon them muft be ftopped at the third Joint above the Bunch, and the others that are for next Year's bearing are to be encouraged in their Growth. The Vine is full of Sap, and if they be not permitted to draw a good Part of it for their Growth, there will be Abundance of ufelefs Shoots fent forth.

Vermin are now frequent, their Summer Brood is come to Growth, and your Fruit are juft in a Condition to be devoured: The carefulleft Eye muft now be kept upon all the Trees; every Morning and Evening let the Owner or Gardiner look for Snails; there will be Abundance of thefe where very few are feen; they hide themfelves fo cunningly that their Mifchief is very eafily feen, when themfelves are fcarce poffible to be found; but the Way is to watch their Time of coming out, this is early and late, when they may be eafily killed in great Numbers, or a warm Shower will bring them out in the Middle of the Day.

Let

Let the Borders about the Fruit Trees be as carefully kept clear of Weeds as thofe where the choiceft Flowers are, and the oftener they are hoed for this Purpofe the better; it not only deftroys all Weeds, but breaks the Surface of the Ground, fo that it the better receives the Dews and gentle Showers for the Refrefhment of the Roots.

No large Plants fhould ever be fuffered to ftand in the fame Borders where Fruit Trees are. This is a common Miftake, from People's thinking the Roots of the Trees go deeper and fhoot farther for their Nourifhment. It is true that they do fo, but there is nothing does them fo much Injury as the choaking them up clofe at the Stem, and about the Circuit of it.

If the Seafon be dry there will be great Advantage in now and then well watering the Wall Trees, efpecially fuch as are young.

S E C T. VIII.

Of the Management of the Farm for the Month of May.

GOOD Weather in *May* is very defireable to the Farmer.

In the Beginning of this Month let him examine his Fields of Barley; if they be too rank the Blades muft be taken off; for this Purpofe he may mow it, or turn in Sheep: In fome Places they venture to turn in Hogs, but this is a very ill Practice.

The quick-growing Barley may be fown this Month.

The

The Sheep are to begin to be folded ; and this is the beſt Time for putting the Mares to the Horſes.

The Beginning of this Month is the beſt Seaſon for ſowing of Buckwheat; and at the ſame Time Flax and Hemp may be ſown, and ſome later Crops of Peaſe.

Milch Cows and fattening Cattle are to be put into freſh Paſtures ; and a particular Care is to be taken of all that regards the Dairy.

This is a very good Seaſon for draining of wet Land.

Let the Farmer alſo now look to his young Quick-ſets and weed them, and turn his Calves to Graſs.

Toward the End of this Month there will be Clover fit for mowing ; and the Farmer who has got into the Improvement of Saintfoin, Lucerne, and the like Graſſes, is to begin mowing the forwarder of them, for they will yield him a great Increaſe, and will ſhoot ſo quick from this mowing that another Crop will be ready preſently.

It is a great Advantage in all theſe which the Farmers call artificial Graſſes, that the Time of cut-ting them is juſt when they are getting into Flower, before the Roots are exhauſted ; they yield the ſweeteſt and beſt Hay at this Time, and their Roots are ready to ſend up a new Crop immediately.

This is a very good Time for ſelling off the Winter fed Cattle.

We have given Directions to the Shepherd in the preceding Pages to beware of the Occaſions of the Rot, and other Diſtempers of Sheep from bad Food, and we are now to repeat the Caution to the Owner, that he look well after them. The latter End of *May* is the Time when the Rot moſtly comes on ; let him therefore take particular Care to guard againſt the Occaſions of it at this Seaſon, and to examine his Sheep from Time to Time, to ſee if any ſuch Thing have happened to them.

When

When he perceives it beginning among them let him remove thofe which are diftempered, that they do not infect the reft, and turn all into a new Pafture.

If the other have been wet, which is commonly the Caufe of this Diforder, let him remove them into a dryer, and let him particularly chufe one where there is Abundance of wild Thyme. We have mentioned the falutary Qualities of this Herb before, and there is nothing in which it is more eminently ufeful than the ftopping a Rot. I have made it an Obfervation, that few Sheep have this terrible Diforder where that grows plentifully among the Paftures, and nothing is a better Prefervative when they are in Danger.

THE